Code-switching

European University Studies

Europäische Hochschulschriften

Publications Universitaires Européennes

Series XXI	**Linguistics**
Reihe XXI	Linguistik
Série XXI	Linguistique

Volume / Band **385**

Baban Mohamed

Code-switching

A Case Study of Kurdish-German
Pre-school Bilingual Children

Bibliographic Information published by the Deutsche Nationalbibliothek
The Deutsche Nationalbibliothek lists this publication in the Deutsche Nationalbibliografie; detailed bibliographic data is available in the internet at http://dnb.d-nb.de.

ISSN 0721-3352
ISBN 978-3-631-64683-0 (Print)
E-ISBN 978-3-653-04202-3 (E-Book)
DOI 10.3726/978-3-653-04202-3

© Peter Lang GmbH
Internationaler Verlag der Wissenschaften
Frankfurt am Main 2014
All rights reserved.
PL Academic Research is an Imprint of Peter Lang GmbH.
Peter Lang – Frankfurt am Main · Bern · Bruxelles · New York · Oxford · Warszawa · Wien

All parts of this publication are protected by copyright. Any utilisation outside the strict limits of the copyright law, without the permission of the publisher, is forbidden and liable to prosecution. This applies in particular to reproductions, translations, microfilming, and storage and processing in electronic retrieval systems.

This publication has been peer reviewed.

www.peterlang.com

Acknowledgements

I am deeply indebted to Univ. Prof. Dr. Wolfgang Grosser for his encouragement, constructive help and belief in me. I want to thank Univ. Prof. Dr. Wilfried Wieden for his class discussions, teaching me to read critically. I would like to thank Dr. Martin Kaltenbacher for his valuable advice, suggestions for improvement, for his patience and for reading innumerable drafts.

I am especially thankful to the parents of my informants in Salzburg and in Vienna, for their warm hospitality and for letting me carry out my observations with their children in their houses. I am also grateful to the teachers at the *Kurdische Schule* in Vienna.

Above all, however, I want to thank my brother Arfan, without his financial support I would not have been able to come to Austria and to do my studies at Salzburg University.

Preface

It is a truism that in our world some form of bilingualism has become part of most people's lives. Nevertheless our knowledge of the processes involved in the acquisition and the use of two or more languages by bilinguals has in many ways remained incomplete. Moreover, most research in the field has focused on adult bilingualism and has little to say about the development of bilingualism in individuals. What is badly needed are accounts of how children develop the functions and roles of different languages and how they manage to keep the language systems apart or switch from one to the other - not arbitrarily or due to a lack of competence as sometimes has been suggested but purposefully and with functions in mind.

Therefore it is of great importance that we have empirical studies such as the one by Baban Mohamed. His focus of interest is on the language behaviour of Kurdish pre-school children in Austria, who were born in Austria and have learnt Kurdish in their families and German through contact with German speaking playmates and in kindergartens. The study, which is a slightly modified version of his MA diploma thesis, shows specific interest in practices of code switching and mixing as displayed by his Kurdish subjects and in how far these can be sufficiently explained by existing models of (adult) bilingual language behavior.

What makes the study specifically interesting is the fact that the two languages involved, Kurdish and German, are typologically different in many parts of their grammatical systems (e.g. suffixation vs. free morphemes, the use of verbal operators, pro-drop parameter etc.). Therefore, the empirical data gathered for the project present the opportunity to evaluate claims about the relevance of grammatical constraints in code-switching that have been brought forward particularly by early researchers, such as Poplack 1980. Concerning these claims the author presents conclusive evidence that linguistic constraints cannot be supported in the light of the data and their context of language use. Myers-Sccotton's Matrix Language Frame Model seems to be better suited to cater for most of the instances of code-switching. Finally, the author is able to show that Kurdish pre-school children perform clear social distinctions in their use of the two languages.

The study presents ample evidence of the fact that the existence of two or more languages in a person is a fascinating phenomenon and rather testifies to humans' linguistic creative capacity than to scenarios suggesting dangers of incomplete language learning. This book should be of interest to everyone interested in bilingualism, language contact phenomena, identity construction of bilingual learners, or (foreign) languages and education.

Wolfgang Grosser
Department of English Studies
Paris-Lodron-University Salzburg

Table of contents

List of tables and figures 15
List of abbreviations 17
0. Introduction 19
    0.1. Aim of the project... 19
    0.2. Motives 19
    0.3. Approach 19
1. Language acquisition and bilingualism 21
    1.1. Describing the phenomenon of bilingualism 21
    1.2. Monolingual vs. bilingual acquisition 21
    1.2.1. Monolingual acquisition 21
    1.2.2. Bilingual acquisition 22
    1.3. Bilingualism 23
    1.3.1. Definitions and descriptions 23
    1.3.2. Types of bilingualism 25
    1.3.2.1. Balanced bilingualism... 25
    1.3.2.2. Semilingualism 26

2. Code-switching (CS) 29
    2.1. Defining the term 29
    2.2. Code-switching vs. code-mixing and other related phenomena 30
    2.2.1. Code mixing 30
    2.2.2. Borrowing 31
    2.2.3. Interference 33
    2.2.4. Transfer... 34
    2.3. Terminology 34
    2.4. Categorization of CS 35

2.4.1. Types of CS 35
2.4.2. Processes of intrasentnetial CS 36

3. Linguistic factors on CS 39
   3.1. Code-switching is not random 39
   3.2. Constraints on CS 40
   3.2.1. Particular grammatical constraints 41
   3.2.1.1. Mahootian (1996) 41
   3.2.1.2. Timm (1975) 42
   3.2.2. General constraints 42
   3.2.2.1. The free morpheme constraint 42
   3.2.2.2. The equivalence constraint 43
   3.3. Theoretical model of intrasentential CS 45
   3.3.1. The Matrix Language Model (ML) 45
   3.3.1.1 Early accounts of the Matrix Language Model 45
   3.3.1.1.1. Joshi: Matrix Language Model (ML) 45
   3.3.1.1.1.1. Closed class vs. open class items 46
   3.3.1.1.1.2. Constraints on closed class items 46
   3.3.1.2. Base language vs. embedded language 47
   3.3.2. Myers-Scotton: Matrix Language Frame Model (MLF) 48
   3.3.2.1. Defining the Matrix Language and the Embedded Language 48
   3.3.2.2. Types of constituents of the MLF Model 49
   3.3.2.3. Content morphemes vs. system morphemes 50
   3.4. Lexical development of bilingual children ....…51

4. Functional factors on CS 53
   4.1. Situational vs. metaphorical switching 53
   4.2. 'We code' vs. 'they code' opposition 54

4.3. The Markedness model 55

5. Speech community 57
   5.1. Use of the term 57
   5.2. Definitions of speech community 57

6. The Study 61
   6.1. The fieldwork: Kurdish immigrant community 61
      6.1.1. An asylum community 62
      6.1.2. The Kurdish speech community 63
   6.2. The languages of this study 64
      6.2.1. Inflectional morphemes 64
      6.2.1.1. Noun inflection / Declension 64
      6.2.1.1.1. Noun inflection in Kurdish 64
      6.2.1.1.1.1. Definition 64
      6.2.1.1.1.2. Number 66
      6.2.1.1.2. Personal pronoun inflection 66
      6.2.1.1.2.1. Personal pronouns 66
      6.2.1.1.3. Nouns with pronominal suffixes 67
      6.2.1.1.2. Noun Inflection in German 68
      6.2.1.2. Verb inflection / Conjugation 68
      6.2.1.2.1. Verb inflection in Kurdish 68
      6.2.1.2.2. Verb inflection in German 69
      6.2.2. Negation 70
      6.2.3. Phrasal structure in Kurdish 71
      6.2.3.1. Nominal phrases 71
      6.2.3.2. Verbal phrase 71
      6.2.3.2.1. Verbal phrases with the Kurdish operator *krdn* 72

6.2.3.3. Prepositional phrase 73
6.2.4. Clause word order 73
6.2.5. Other phenomena 75
6.2.5.1. Pro-drop / Null-subject parameter 75
6.2.5.2. Case morphology 76
6.2.5.3. Gender distinction 76

7. Subjects and recordings 79
7.1. Method of observation 79
7.2. Subjects 80
7.3. Recordings 80

8. Kurdish-German intrasentential CS: data and analysis 83
8.1. What is not accounted as CS 83
8.2. The data 84
8.3. Data analysis 86
8.3.1. Categories switched 86
8.3.1.1. Noun 86
8.3.1.2. Verb 87
8.3.1.3. Adverb 88
8.3.1.4. Preposition 89
8.3.2. Affixation of Kurdish morphemes to German lexemes 90
8.3.2.1. German noun plus Kurdish suffixes 90
8.3.2.2. Kurdish-German compound verbs 92
8.3.3. Compound verbs in the CS literature 93
8.3.4. What is special about German-Kurdish compound verbs? ... 95
8.3.5. Summary 96

9. Constraints on Kurdish-German CS data 97
   9.1. Universal constraints 97
      9.1.1. The free morpheme constraint 97
      9.1.2. The equivalence constraint 100
   9.2. The closed class constraint 101
   9.3. Applying Myers-Scotton's MLF model to the data 103
      9.3.1. Identifying the Matrix Language (ML) in the data 104
      9.3.1.1. The frequency counting criterion 104
      9.3.1.2. Language proficiency 106
      9.3.2. Separating content and system morphemes 106
      9.3.3. The Matrix Language hypothesis 107
      9.3.4. The dominant-language hypothesis (Petersen 1988) 111
      9.3.5. Criterion for identifying the ML in the data 112
      9.3.6. Summary of linguistic constraints on Kurdish-German CS 113

10. Functional factors on Kurdish-German CS 115
   10.1. Data classification 115
   10.2. CS indexing rejection and anger 118
   10.3. Home language 119
   10.4. 'Children code' versus 'parents code' 120
   10.5. The unmarked codes of home interaction 123

11. Conclusion 127

12. Bibliography 131

13. Appendix 139

List of tables and figures

Table 1 Speech situations of the recordings
Table 2 Frequency of codes of communication

Figure 1 Intrasentential code-switches
Figure 2 Intra-word code-switches
Figure 3 The Free Morpheme Constraint
Figure 4 Average number of Kurdish, German and CS turns
Figure 5 Frequency of the three codes: Kurdish (K), German (G) and CS
Figure 6 Frequency of codes of interaction according to the age of interlocutors

Abbreviations

{0}	Uninflected item
1st sg.	First person singular
1st pl.	First person plural
Art.	Article
Aux.	Auxiliary
Adv.	Adverb
Adj.	Adjective
Conj.	Conjunction
CS	Code-switching
Df.	Definite suffix
EL	Embedded Language
G	German
Inf.	Infinitive
Infl.	Inflection, inflected morpheme
Indf.	Indefinite suffix
K	Kurdish
L1	First language
L2	Second language
LI	Lexical Item
ML	Matrix Language
N	Noun
Neg.	Negation
Obj.	Object
Op.	Operator
Pl.	Plural
Prep.	Preposition
Pron.	Pronoun
Poss.	Possessive
Sg.	Single

Suff.	Suffix
Subj.	Subject
V	Verb

0. Introduction

0.1. Aim of the project

This book addresses the phenomenon of code-switching within the field of child bilingualism from both linguistic and sociolinguistic perspectives. Based on collected data from Kurdish-German pre-school bilingual children in Austria, this book aims at giving an analysis of linguistic and extra-linguistic factors that constrain code-switching.

Researchers have found that code-switches are not distributed randomly in sentences but rather occur at specific points. The main questions which this study addresses are the following:

How do bilingual children combine elements from two languages when processing mixed sentences? In other words, how do sections of grammars of two languages overlap in code-switching processes?
What kinds of elements do bilingual children switch?

How do extra-linguistic aspects of bilingualism such as sociolinguistic and psycholinguistic factors influence code-switching?
Why do bilingual children switch at all?

0.2. Motives

The subject of code-switching is of personal relevance to me insofar as I am a foreign student at Salzburg university and a member of an immigrant community in Austria, and the subject is of general relevance since today a high percentage of the world's population is bilingual; bilingualism has become and will continue to be part of most people's lives.

0.3. Approach

This book will be divided into a theoretical part and an empirical part. While the first part outlines a theoretical background on bilingualism and code-switching, the second part is devoted to the application of the theory to the data of the study, namely Kurdish-German child code-switching data.

Chapter 1 and 2 will introduce the key terms of the study, namely language acquisition, bilingualism and code-switching. Different definitions and interpretations of these terms that have been put forward in research will be discussed and compared so as to clearly state which definition of each of these terms are being used in this book. However, since each of these terms offers a vast field of investigation and the terms are too broad, this study will concentrate on one very specific phenomenon observed in connection with bilinguals, namely code-switching.

In chapter 3, which forms the main section of the theoretical part of the book, a discussion of linguistic constraints on code-switching will be presented. Several linguistic constraints and theoretical models of code-switching will be presented and opposed to each other. However, particular focus in this chapter will be put on one specific theoretical model of code-switching, which is the Matrix Language Frame Model (MLF) by Myers-Scotton.

Chapter 4 will present a discussion of functional factors in code-switching. This chapter will address some of the social and psychological factors that involve and influence the occurrence of code-switching. Furthermore some social norms that constrain the choice of languages by bilingual speakers will be discussed.

Chapter 5 deals with the concept of speech community; a brief discussion of the concept from both linguistic and sociolinguistic perspectives will be presented. Further, definitions and the use of the term 'speech community' by the scholars will be introduced.

In chapter 6 and the following chapters a new study on child code-switching will be presented. Information about the two languages involved will be given at the beginning. Furthermore in chapter 7 the subjects, their immigrant community and methodological aspects will be presented before the actual corpus of intrasentential code-switching data will be introduced (in chapter 8). It will be followed by testing different grammatical constraints on the data. Furthermore theoretical constructs and hypotheses of the Matrix Language Frame (MLF) model will be applied to the data of the study (in chapter 9).

The final chapter of the book (chapter 10) will be devoted to analyse functional factors in the collected data. The collected data will be classified in order to give an analysis on functional factors of code-switching to find out when, how and why children code-switch.

1. Language acquisition and bilingualism
1.1. Describing the phenomenon of bilingualism

Bilingualism is not a phenomenon that concerns only a few special people. In fact, as Wei (2000: 5) argues, one in three of the world's population routinely uses two or more languages for work, family life and leisure. The state of acquiring more than one language by a child or an adult is not the exception, an issue concerning only a few learners; it is rather an everyday reality for a quite substantial part of today's society. In Austria, for example, according to the Austrian Statistical Bureau, in Mid-2006, 814,800 foreigners legally lived in Austria, representing 9.8% of the total population. In Vienna, in 2005 more than 30% of the population was either foreign or of foreign origin (Wikipedia, 2010). Thus, the statistics show that bilingualism is the normal and rather natural state of being for a substantial part of the people living in Austria.

On the other hand, the investigation of bilingualism is a broad complex phenomenon that includes the study of the nature of the individual bilingual's knowledge and use of two languages as well as the broader social and psychological consequences of using more than a language in a given society.

1.2. Monolingual vs. bilingual acquisition
1.2.1. Monolingual acquisition

Generally speaking, in early studies of language acquisition the focus was on monolingual acquisition and not on bilingual acquisition. Before research on bilingualism was being established, the scope of reference for the study of language for establishing the linguistic theory has been primarily devoted to the topic of monolingualism and the theory of monolingual language acquisition.

From the early nineteenth century there was even a widespread belief that bilingualism had a negative effect on a human being's intellectual and spiritual growth. Thus, relying upon such views and referring to some of the early research on bilingualism in childhood, some studies concluded that "bilingual children possess below average vocabularies in both languages and even their combined vocabulary is generally inferior to the vocabulary of their monolingual counterparts" (Ausubel, Sullivan, and Ives 1980, cited in Palij and Homel 1987: 131). Moreover, research on language acquisition has been dominated by Chomsky's view that linguistic theory should be concerned "with an ideal speaker-listener, in a completely homogeneous speech community, who knows its language perfectly" (Chomsky 1965: 3).

There were a number of reasons for putting less focus on studding bilingual acquisition, Bhatia and Ritchie (1988: 569) point out that the view has predominated that the phenomenon of bilingualism is highly complex and therefore its study must await the satisfactory development of a theory of monolingual language acquisition. It was argued that it is not wise to invest time in the study of the bilingual child because there are fundamental theoretical problems with defining and measuring the phenomenon of bilingualism. Ultimately, bilingualism has been studied less extensively than monolingualism and an outcome of this situation is- as Grosjean (2004: 32) points out- that research dealing with bilinguals has often produced conflicting results as some studies in the field of language development have found evidence that children who acquire two languages simultaneously go through a fusion stage while others have questioned this stage.

1.2.2. Bilingual acquisition

In contradiction to the common belief that bilingualism has a negative effect on bilingual children since they would be inferior to monolingual children on most measures of verbal intelligence, other researchers discovered that bilingualism does not harm the speech development or the general mental development of the children. In the late 1940s and early 1950s, scholars in the United States established the dimensions of the field of bilingualism and language contact. Since then up to the present day, the study of bilingualism has been getting more attention and the field is ever growing.

Leopold (1971: 141), for instance, even seems to have found some advantages for bilingualism in his study of the speech of a bilingual child, as the bilingual child can separate the word from its meaning and focus his attention on the meaning behind the phonetic configurations. The author states "the most striking effect of bilingualism was a noticeable looseness of the link between phonetic word and its meaning. The child never insisted on stereotype wording of stories, as monolingual children often do, and even made vocabulary substitutions freely in memorised rhymes and songs".

As another example, Peal and Lambert (Lambert 1977: 15) in their detailed study of comparing bilingual and monolingual children on various measures of intelligence and achievement in Montreal schools discovered that the bilingual group performed significantly better than the monolingual children, and this led them to conclude that the performance advantages shown by the bilingual children might be the result of greater mental flexibility and a more diversified structure of intellect. What surprised them was that "the French-English bilingual children scored significantly ahead of carefully matched monolinguals on both verbal and nonverbal measures of intelligence" (Lambert 1977: 16).

Among others, these findings led scholars to criticize the early theoretical approaches on language acquisition that focused less extensively on bilingual acquisition. For instance, Haugen (1978: 46) criticizes the theoretical approach that excludes the importance of studies on bilingualism and he argues that such a theoretical concern has left little room for the kind of heterogeneity that characterized bilinguals.

1.3. Bilingualism

1.3.1. Definitions and descriptions

There is no widely accepted definition or measure of bilingualism and bilinguals, including bilingualism in children. There are even fundamental conceptual disagreements and problems with the definition and measurement of bilinguals and the phenomenon of bilingualism.

In very broad terms, the word bilingual describes someone who possesses two languages or more. But the degree of bilingualism and the ability of the bilingual to have equal competence and proficiency in both languages have always been a controversial issue. Moreover, questions have been raised about the criteria on measuring the degree of bilingualism, such as should bilingualism be measured by how fluent people are in two languages, or should only those people be regarded as bilinguals who have equal competence in both languages (Wie 2000: 5). Generally speaking, earlier definitions tended to restrict bilingualism to equal mastery of two languages, while later definitions have accepted much greater variation in bilinguals' competence.

Bilingualism had long been defined as the equal mastery of two languages. This view can be found in earlier linguistic literature, notably in Bloomfield's assertion (Bloomfield 1933: 55) that in cases of language shift in the children of immigrants "where perfect foreign-language learning is not accompanied by loss of the native language, it results in bilingualism, native-like control of two languages". This means that bilinguals are only those people who grow up with two languages and they have full command of these languages. Such definition suggests that the criterion for bilingualism should be native-like control of both languages which results from the addition of a perfectly learned foreign language to one's mother language. However, this early definition of seeing bilingualism as the ability of using two languages equally well has been questioned.

Since bilingualism is a wide spread phenomenon and quite hard to be measured, Bloomfield's definition of the term bilingual, including only 'perfect bilinguals', has been criticized by researchers for being an extreme position towards language acquisition. Haugen (1978: 3) describes Bloomfield's definition as a limited and absolutistic conception that puts bilingualism in a paradoxical position. Haugen further argues and states, "if a speaker is bilingual, he must then be indistinguishable from natives of each language; if he is distinguishable he cannot be a bilingual". Other scholars, Bhatia and Ritchie (1988: 571) for instance, stress that full native control of two languages represents an ideal form of bilingualism that is rarely achieved. However, other scholars take different approaches to define bilingualism as individuals or groups of people who obtain communicative skills, with various degrees of proficiency, in oral and/ or written forms, in order to interact with speakers of one or more languages in a given society. A broad definition of bilingualism is assumed in considering any one who actively uses two languages at some level of proficiency to be bilingual.

Summing up, Hamers and Blanc (1989: 7) argue that all such definitions, which range from native-like competence in two languages to minimal proficiency in a second language, raise a number of theoretical and methodological difficulties. They review the weaknesses of these approaches from two important aspects of bilingualism, which are competence and dimensions of bilingualism. Both mentioned authors argue that these definitions do not specify what is meant by native-like competence, which varies considerably within a multilingual population. They bring examples to support their argument, such as whether a bilingual who possesses very high competence in a second language without necessarily being perceived as a native speaker on account of a foreign accent can be regarded as a bilingual or not. The second point of their criticism is that these definitions refer only to the level of proficiency in both languages, thus ignoring other non-linguistic dimensions of bilingualism.

1.3.2. Types of bilingualism

Various types of bilingualism according to various criteria have been suggested by many linguists. Reflecting on the relationship between age and language acquisition, Meisel (2004: 105) deduces from the critical period hypothesis that one should distinguish between three types of bilingual acquisition:

1) Simultaneous acquisition of bilingualism, if the child begins to acquire two or more languages during the first three or four years of life.
2) Child second language acquisition, if the onset of acquisition of the second or further languages happens between ages five and ten.
3) Adult L2 acquisition, if the acquisition of L2 starts after the age of ten.

However, from another prescriptive, bilingualism has been classified according to the influence of both languages; balanced bilingualism and semilingualism have been suggested. In the following sections several distinctions between these two different types of bilinguals will be compared and close attention will be paid to semilingualism that seems to apply better to the fieldwork of this thesis.

1.3.2.1. Balanced bilingualism

Since bilingualism is a multi-dimensional phenomenon, researchers classify the phenomenon of bilingualism depending on the dimension which they focus on. For example, the distinction between balanced and dominant bilinguals has been made which is based on the relationship between the proficiencies of the languages that bilinguals master. Balanced bilinguals are those who acquire similar degrees of proficiency in both languages, i.e. the bilinguals possess native-like competence in both languages, whereas dominant bilinguals are individuals whose proficiency in one language is higher than that in the other language. From a psycholinguistic perspective, a distinction is made between compound and coordinate language systems; in a compound system, two sets of linguistic signs come to be associated with the same set of meanings, whereas in a coordinate system, translation equivalents in the two languages correspond to two different sets of representations.

Edwards (1994: 58) reflecting on the degree of fluency, refers to the term of semibilingualism. He distinguishes between receptive (passive) bilingualism and productive (active) competence; the difference is between those who understand a language- either spoken or written- but cannot produce it themselves, and those who can do both. A receptive competence has been referred to as semibilingualism that should not be confused with semilingualism, which refers to a lack of complete fluency in either language.

1.3.2.2. Semilingualism

Semilingualism refers to a situation where bilingual children possess less than native-like skills in both languages, i.e. lack of complete fluency in either language. Seminligualism occurs when one language becomes dominant over the other language. However, the dominance of a language of the bilingual may change with context over time or across place.

This type of bilingualism can be found amongst migrant children. Romaine (1989: 167), for instance, classifies the main types of bilingualism depending on factors such as the native languages of parents and the language of the community at large. One of her classifications of early childhood bilingualism, which corresponds better with the field work of this study, has been classified as the following:

- 'Non-dominant home language without community support'.

In this type of bilingualism, which forms the focus of this study, the parents share the same native language but the dominant language of the community at large is not that of the parents. And the parents' strategy is to speak their own language to the child.

Other researchers refer to such a situation that reflects the different social pressures and needs on the bilinguals as subtractive bilingualism. Edwards (1994:10) distinguishes between additive and subtractive bilingualism; additive bilingualism refers to a situation where both languages continue to be useful and valued, whereas, subtractive bilingualism, on the other hand, often implies a society in which one language is valued more than the other, where one dominates the other.

Furthermore, it has been argued that in a transitional bilingual community where there is unequal status between the bilingual's two languages, one language replaces the other. Fishman (1972: 140) distinguishes between stable and transitional bilingualism and in the latter the acquisition of a second language would eventually displace the first. Fishman emphasizes that due to sociopsychological factors such as favouring one linguistic system over the other, or because of input relationships, like unequal exposure to the two languages over time, one system invariably holds the upper hand over the other and consequently one of the bilingual child's languages becomes dominant. Fishman (1972: 140) states; "if the roles [of languages] were not kept separate by the power of their association with quite separate though complementary values, domains of activity and everyday situations, one language would displace the other".

2. Code-switching (CS)

A central question in the field of bilingualism concerns the interaction between the bilingual's two language systems, including the influence that each system has on the knowledge and use of the other as well as the form and motivation for using both languages in the same discourse, namely code-switching (hereafter CS). CS is most frequently found and studied in the natural speech of members of minority groups who speak the native tongue at home and use the majority language in society at large when dealing with members of groups other than their own.

2.1. Defining the term

Generally, CS is defined as the use of two or more languages in the same discourse, i.e. the use of two or more linguistic varieties in the same conversation, without prominent phonological assimilation of one variety to the other. An early quite influential definition is that of Gumperz (1982: 59), who defines CS as "the juxtaposition within the same speech exchange of passages of speech belonging to two different grammatical systems or subsystems". Similarly, Poplack (1980: 583) in a study on Spanish-English CS defines CS as the alternation of two languages within a single discourse, sentence or constituent. Joshi (1985: 190) describes CS as a systematic and rule-governed phenomenon that refers to a situation where in the course of an utterance speakers of certain bilingual communities systematically produce utterances in which they switch from one language to another possibly several times. More specifically De Houwer (1995, 247) defines CS as follows "It involves the use of elements from two languages within one utterance, conversational turn, or longer stretch of discourse".

Some researchers expand the definition by saying that switching does not only occur in bilingual, but also in monolingual conversations and communities. Romaine (1989: 111), for instance, uses the term CS as it is defined by Gumperz in a more general sense to refer not only to different languages, but also to varieties of the same language as well as styles within a language.

Another influential definition was proposed by Myers-Scotton (1993: 3) within her description of the *matrix language model*. She defines CS as the "selections by bilinguals or multilinguals of forms from an embedded variety in utterances of a matrix variety during the same conversation". In this model, the utterances from another language, which is called embedded language, are embedded in a main- or matrix language.

2.2. Code-switching vs. code-mixing and other related phenomena

In the study of language contact and especially in CS research there has been little agreement on the appropriate definitions of various effects of language contact. So as to make the concept of CS explicit, in the following sections the term CS will be compared with and discussed in relation to some other related phenomena of language contact situations.

2.2.1. Code mixing

As can be seen from the definitions of CS, there is not always consensus about the description of switching. While some scholars doubt the usefulness of making a distinction between CS and code-mixing, others find such a distinction controversial and important. However, there is a great deal of disagreement between the researchers as to what determines clear-cut instances of CS and code-mixing.

Some authors prefer using the term CS instead of code-mixing for some cases of CS. In their distinction between these two terms, Ritchie and Bhatia (2004: 337) use the term CS to refer to the use of various linguistic units such as words, phrases, clauses, and sentences primarily from two participating grammatical systems across sentence boundaries within a speech event. Thus CS, in their words, is intersentential and is motivated by social and psychological factors, as illustrated in (1).

Ex. 1

| The three old ones spoke nothing but Spanish. *No hablaban ingles.* | 'The three old ones spoke nothing but Spanish. *They didn't speak English*' |

(Gumperz 1982, cited in Ritchie and Bhatia 2004: 345)

In (1) the first sentence has occurred in English while the second utterance of the same speech event occurred in Spanish. Ritchie and Bhatia (2004: 345) use the term of CS to refer to the case of switching in (1). The authors further argue that the CS in (1) where the message expressed in one language has been repeated with some modification in the other language illustrate the emphatic and clarificatory function of CS.

Code-mixing, as the authors argue, refer to the mixing of various linguistic units like morphemes, words, modifiers, phrases, clauses and sentences primarily from two participating grammatical systems within a sentence. In their terminology, code-mixing is intrasentential and is constrained by grammatical principles.

In contrary to the above discussion, Muysken (2000: 1) uses the term cod-mixing to refer to all cases where lexical items and grammatical features from two languages appear in one sentence. The author, thus, employs code-mixing as the generic term, being more neutral, and CS for rapid succession of several languages in a single speech event.

2.2.2. Borrowing

Some studies claim that CS must be separated from borrowing and these studies seriously consider the CS versus borrowing question. Most researchers find it important and appropriate to distinguish between the two. There has been, however, little agreement as to how the distinction is to be made. For this purpose, some possible criteria such as degree of assimilation of borrowed forms and the frequency of occurrence of the items have been suggested and discussed by researchers. Along these arguments, however, it is also mentioned that the problem of distinguishing borrowings from CS can be complex, especially if the studies rely on purely linguistic criteria. As Poplack (1988: 220) indicates, with the smaller switched constitute, particularly at the level of the lone lexical item it will be more difficult to resolve the question of whether we are dealing with a code-switch or a loanword, as borrowing is constrained differently from CS.

In general terms, borrowing is referred to as a word and clause level phenomenon, whereas CS is a conversational phenomenon of utterance level. Gumperz (1982: 66), for instance, draws a distinction between these two terms and defines borrowing as "the introduction of single words, or short, frozen, idiomatic phrases from one variety into the other". On the other hand, CS, as Gumperz further argues relies on the meaningful juxtaposition of what speakers must consciously or subconsciously process as strings formed according to the internal rules of two distinct grammatical systems. This distinction proposes that in the case of borrowing, loans tend to follow the grammatical rule of the new language and the elements associated with one language are assimilated into the grammatical system of the other language as illustrated in (2).

Ex. 2

Er hat das *gefixt*	He *fixed* it

German-English, Gumperz (1982: 67)

In (2) the English verb *fix* has been inserted into a German utterance. Gumperz argues that this shows a case of borrowing, where the lexical root *fix* has been borrowed from English into German, and that the borrowed verb *fix* has taken on German prefixes and suffixes. Similarly, according to Poplack CS operates on the grammatical constraints of both languages, while borrowing is constrained grammatically by the recipient language.

However, a different position is held by Myers-Scotten (1988: 159), who points to the problem of distinguishing CS from borrowing and argues against resolving this problem on a structural basis, i.e. considering degrees of assimilation. In her argument, Myers-Scotten falsifies the hypothesis that borrowed morphemes are more phonologically assimilated into the first language (L1) than switched morphemes and so as to support this claim, she uses an African data base that provides her with many clear established borrowings that show little assimilation as illustrated in the following example.

Ex. 3

Town [taun] 'city center' shows next to no assimilation as a common loan into diverse Kenyan African languages spoken in Nairobi.

Myers-Scotten (1988: 159)

As a possible solution, Myers-Scotten proposes that the problem of distinguishing borrowing and CS can be solved if it is approached in terms of social content, not structure. She further explains that, as an example, all phonological features in a social dialect are not distinctive and are therefore no crucial defining features of the dialect. Those features which carry social significance in a negotiation, Myers-Scotten claims, constitute CS, while those which do not, are borrowings.

Importantly, Myers-Scotten's Matrix Language-Frame (MLF) model (see 3.3.2) proposes an important frame for distinguishing borrowing from CS, which has the matrix language providing the morphosyntactic frame of mixed constituent in a code-switched utterance. Hence, if we apply Poplack's distinction of borrowing and CS to the MLF Model, then the matrix language grammatically constrains borrowing, while CS should be operated on the grammatical constraints of both participating languages of a switched utterance.

2.2.3. Interference

Other terms have also been suggested by researchers to be distinguished from the CS phenomenon. For instance, insisting on a distinction between borrowing as a process of code-alternation and switching as a process of code-preservation, Haugen (1978: 21) proposes that CS be used to refer to the alternate use of two languages, including everything from the introduction of a single, unassimilated word up to a complete sentence or more into the context of another language. On the other hand, in the case of overlapping systems Haugen accepts the term interference for the simultaneous overlapping of two norms, as it occurs when bilinguals are unable or unwilling to keep the codes entirely separate.

Musyken (2004: 147) differentiates between the fields of CS, including code mixing, and morpho-syntactic interference. In the case of CS or code-mixing, as he points out, there is lexical material from two languages present in the clause, in addition to morpho-syntactic structure from both languages, as illustrated in (4).

Ex. 4

| Weet je *what she is doing*? | Do you know *what she is doing*? |

English-Dutch, Crama and van Gelderen 1984, cited in Musyken (2004: 148)

As the author argues, the example in (4) shows a case of CS from Dutch into English; the utterance starts out with Dutch and at the point of *what* switches to English. Interference, on the other hand, involves morpho-syntactic structures from two languages but lexical material from only one of them. As an example, Musyken (2004: 150) points to the varieties of German and Dutch spoken by

Turkish immigrants that show a greater range of null subject constructions than native German and Dutch.

2.2.4. Transfer

Some researchers contrast CS with transfer. Clyne (2000: 258), for instance, refers to CS as a situation where the speaker stops using language A and uses language B, so that the syntactic connections are now based on the speaker's language B, whereas in transfer a single item is transferred from language B to A or vice versa. The author further argues that in a sentence where the verb alone is inserted from language A into language B, it could be regarded as an unintegrated lexical transfer rather than CS, as illustrated in (5). In other cases where there is phonological integration, it can be regarded as stabilized lexical transfer.

Ex. 5

The dog *corria* quickly down the street	The dog *rans* quickly down the street

Portuguese-English, Klavans 1983, cited in Clyne (2000: 258)

Auer (2000: 170) distinguishes these two terms from a very different point of view of what has been proposed by Clyne and some others. Summarizing some of the main findings of an analysis on CS and transfer that he carried out in Germany among the children of Italian migrant workers, Auer uses the term *language alternation* to cover both terms of CS and transfer. CS, as he argues, refers to a situation where the language alternation in question is connected to a particular point, whereas transfer does not relate to a certain point in conversation but to a certain well defined unit, for example a word, a sentence, or a language unit. Auer concludes that a high degree of lexical transfer can be noted in the analysis which is not usually adapted to the phonology or grammar of the receiving language, and interestingly, he stresses that it would be mistaken to speak of a receiving language there at all.

2.3. Terminology

As a conclusion about a concrete definition and description of the term CS and also to avoid any ambiguity in applying the term to the collected data of this study, I would rather prefer to focus on the point that both terms of CS and code-mixing can be found in the types of CS that will be discussed in the following section. Some studies make a distinction between CS and code-mixing on the basis of whether it is intersentential or intrasentential. Code-mixing would then be intrasentential switching- as it has been called by some researchers such as Appel and Muysken (1987: 121) and Muysken (2000: 3) - and CS would be intersentenial switching. So, throughout the scope of this study, the term CS will have the sense of intersentential and intrasentential switching and the term code-mixing will not be used.

2.4. Categorization of CS

In this section different types of CS will be presented and explained. However, three different processes will be classified that are argued to be occurred in intrasentential CS.

2.4.1. Types of CS

In an early classification of CS, Poplack (1980) distinguishes three types of switching which include tag-switching, intersentential and intrasentential CS. Romaine (1989, 112) defines and explains each type as follows.

- Tag-switching: It refers to the insertion of a tag in one language into an utterance which is otherwise entirely in the other language, e.g. *you know*, *I know*, etc., as some English examples and the rest is in the other language.

- Intersentential switching: It refers to a switch at a clause or sentence boundary, where each clause or sentence is in one language or another. It requires greater fluency in both languages than tag-switching, as illustrated in (6).

Ex. 6

Sometimes I'll start a sentence in English *y terminó in espannol*
'Sometimes I'll start a sentence in English *and finish it in Spanish*'

Spanish-English (Polack 1980: 581)

- Intrasentential switching: it refers to switching of different types that occur within the clause or sentence boundary as in (7).

Ex. 7

| 'You'll buy *xune-ye jaedid*' | 'You'll buy *a new house*' |

Farsi-English (Mahootian 1993: 390)

In the description of intrasentential CS, Romaine (1989: 113) argues that switching may also include mixing within word boundaries. In a research that she conducted on CS and language mixing in a Panjabi-speaking community in Birmingahm, she gets English words with Panjabi inflectional morphology such as *shoppa* (shops). This type of switching involves the greatest syntactic risk that may be avoided by most fluent bilinguals, a view which has been put forward by Poplack and reargued by Romanie. The grammar of intrasentential CS has been further discussed by other researchers as well. For instance, Myers-Scotten and Jake (2000: 281) insist that only in intrasentential CS the grammars of the two languages are in contact. The two languages involved do not participate equally. One language which sets the grammatical frame is more dominant. They also support Romaine's argument that the speaker may avoid those intrasentential switches which are syntactically risky. This might assure grammatical utterances, as they claim.

Since the major issue of this book is about the constraints on the intrasentential type of CS, the main focus of the rest of the theoretical part of this book will be devoted to intrasentential type of CS.

2.4.2. Processes of intrasentnetial CS

Muysken (2000: 3) in his detailed study on intrasentential CS argues that several distinct processes are at work in intrasentnetial CS. However, the author avoids using the term code-switching and prefers using the term code-mixing to refer to all cases where lexical items and grammatical features from two languages appear in one sentence. The author classifies three different processes or types of CS that occur in intrasentential CS.

- Insertion: this type involves the embedding of a constituent, either a single-word or a multiple-word item, usually in a nested ABA structure (A and B designating the two languages).

Ex. 8

| Yo anduve *in a state of shock* por dos dias | 'I walked *in a state of shock* for two days' |

Spanish-English, cited in Muysken (2000: 5)

- Alternation: It refers to the process of alternation between structures from languages. This is where two languages remain relatively separate.

Ex. 9

| Marr hoeft niet, *li-anna ida seft ana...* | 'But it needs not be, *for when I see, I...* |

Moroccan Arabic-Dutch, cited in Muysken (2000: 5)

- Congruent lexicalization: This is the third category which refers to a situation where the two languages share a grammatical structure which can be filled lexically with elements from each language and there is planning in both languages simultaneously.

Ex. 10

| Wett jij [whaar] Jenny *is*? | 'Do you know where Jenny *is*? |

English-Dutch, cited in Muysken (2000: 5)

These terms have been applied to CS studies by other scholars as well. Backus (2004: 701) for instance, uses the terms insertion and alternation to analyse his Turkish-Dutch CS data collected in 1996. Insertion, as Backus points out, involves the use of single Embedded Language (EL) words in Matrix Language (ML) clauses (see 3.3.2.1. for these terms). This is illustrated in (11), where the language of the clause, in structural terms, is Turkish throughout.

Ex. 11

Mesela okul-da iki tane kiz da bana *verkering* sor-du
'For instance, two girls at school have asked me out on *a daté*'

Turkish-Dutch, Backus (2004: 701)

Alternation, on the other hand, is the actual switching of languages at sentence or clause boundaries. Backus shows this in (12), where the first clause is Turkish and the second is Dutch.

Ex. 12

Sen de kalkman lazim onlarla *en hoe moet je dan op de rest letten*?
'You must get up with them as well, *and then how can you keep an eye on the rest?*'

Turkish-Dutch, Backus (2004: 701)

3. Linguistic factors on CS

In general, studies on bilingualism and CS deal with the description and analysis of CS from two different perspectives. Various studies show that the occurrence of CS is governed by both structural intra-linguistic factors and extra-linguistic factors such as social and situational.

A range of literature on CS focuses on social and pragmatic functions of CS. It has been recognized that a variety of social factors constrain CS, such as setting, topic and degree of competence in both languages. However, the grammatical perspective is primarily concerned with accounting for the linguistic constraints on CS, and for this purpose researchers try to formulate general constraints on CS. In this regard, studies try to describe the nature of bilingual grammar and to find out how two grammatical systems of a bilingual's two languages interact.

In this chapter and also in chapter 4, both linguistic and extra-linguistic factors of CS will be discussed in detail. First, the focus of the theoretical discussion will be on the more purely linguistic factors. Second, in chapter 4, attention will be paid to the social and functional factors of CS which, by some researchers, are considered as the strongest constraints on the occurrence of CS.

The two chapters aim to incorporate both linguistic and functional factors into a possible single model to account for CS behaviour. As researchers argue, it is only by linking ethnographic behaviour with linguistic analysis that CS behaviour can be most adequately explained.

3.1. Code-switching is not random

Scholars researching CS stress that the phenomenon of CS is not arbitrary or random but must follow certain rules.

Although in some of the earlier literature the occurrence of CS was characterised as random with no syntactic restrictions on where switching can occur, most investigators now appear to agree that in many aspects CS is rule-governed and they suggest syntactic constraints on CS (Poplack 1988: 227).

Thus, most studies on CS especially from the 1980s consider CS as a type of skilled performance with social motivations. Gumperz (1982: 72), for instance, investigating Spanish-English CS argues that the language mixture is not random but that the motivation for CS seems to be stylistic and metaphorical rather than grammatical. Joshi (1985: 190) describes the characteristics of intrasentential CS, whereby the mixed utterances are spoken without hesitation, pauses, repetitions, etc. He suggests that CS is not random interference of one system with the other, but rather it seems to be due to systematic interactions between the two systems. Similarly, Ritchie and Bhatia (2004: 338) point to Labov's statement on the Spanish-English mixing on the part of New York Puerto Rican bilingual speakers, which- according to Labov- must be described as a "strange mixture of the two languages" which is not subject to constraints, Ritchie and Bhatia stress that there is now unanimous consensus among linguists and other scholars that language switching behaviour of bilinguals is systematic but complex.

In a large number of studies which analyse specific cases of intra-sentential CS from a grammatical perspective, it has been found that intra-sentential code-switches are not distributed randomly in the sentences, but rather occur at specific points. Where much less agreement has been reached is with respect to general properties of the process of CS.

In the following sections of this chapter, different constraints and models will be presented, which try to explain or predict CS.

3.2. Constraints on CS

In broad terms, researchers take different approaches aiming at formulating constraints on CS. Some early studies have tried to articulate constraints on switching from the surface word order, from class, or size of switched material. Hence, various linguistic constraints on the basis of various linguistic corpora have been proposed which describe grammatical possibilities or impossibilities to switch at certain positions in a sentence. In contrary to this approach, recent scholars - Myers-Scotton (1993) among others- claim that the grammatical theory should primarily focus on relations below the sentence level. It is argued that only at the intrasentential level researchers are able to observe with some certainty the interaction between two grammatical systems.

3.2.1. Particular grammatical constraints
3.2.1.1. Mahootian (1996)

Relying on general principles of phrase structure rather than on constraints specific to CS, Mahootian (1996: 387) argues that the same rules that apply to monolingual utterances apply to code-switched utterances. She proposes a principle that defines syntactic CS boundaries as below;

- The language of a head determines the syntactic properties of its complements in CS and monolingual contexts alike.

According to this principle, as the author explains, phrasal heads impose their syntactic requirements on their complements, determining the phrase structure position, category, and feature content of their complements. She argues that the principle extends to all syntactic heads whether lexical or functional, including determiners, complementizers, case-marking morphemes and inflectional elements. Mahootian uses a corpus of Farsi-English CS data which she collected from spontaneous speech. She observes that the language of the verb determines the placement of the object, as illustrated in the following example.

Ex. 13

You'll buy *xune-ye jaedid*	'You'll buy *a new house*'

Farsi-English, Mahootian (1993b, cited in Mahootian 1996: 390)

The principle predicts that code-switched sequences, in which an English verb follows a Farsi object, as in (14), will not occur and the author finds no such switches reported in the literature.

Ex. 14

*You *xune-ye jaedid* will buy	'You *house-a new* will buy ' 'You will buy *a new house*'

Farsi-English, Mahhotian (1996: 391)

3.2.1.2. Timm (1975)

Timm (1975, cited in Appel and Muysken 1987: 122), proposes some constraints on CS as follows;

- Subject and object pronouns must be in the same language as the main verb, as illustrated in (15).

Ex. 15

| *Mira him | 'Look at him' |

- An auxiliary and a main verb, or a main verb and an infinitive must be in the same language, as in (16).

Ex. 16

| *They want a venir | 'They want to come' |

3.2.2. General constraints

3.2.2.1. The free morpheme constraint

In her investigation of a stable bilingual Puerto Rican community in New York, Poplack (1980: 585) makes the first systematic attempt to formulate general syntactic constraints on CS. She proposes that Spanish-English CS can be generated by a model of grammar which is governed by two constraints.

The first of these is the *free morpheme* constraint, which proposes that a switch may not occur between a bound morpheme and a lexical form unless the latter has been phonologically integrated into the language of the bound morpheme", (Poplack 1980: 585). As illustrated in (17).

Ex. 17

| *Eat-*iendo* | 'Eat-*ing*' |

Spanish-English, Poplack 1980: 585)

The item in (17), where the Spanish bound morpheme {–*iendo*} {'-ing'} is affixed to the English root 'eat', as Poplack argues, has not been attested in the study of CS, unless one of the morphemes has been integrated phonologically into the language of the other.

Proposing a constraint in such a theoretical sense, contrary to the descriptive sense, as MacSwan (2004: 285) points out, applies to a system of linguistic rules and attempts to capture a range of linguistic facts.

However, the *free morpheme constraint* has been controversial. While it is supported in numerous corpora, other scholars claim to have identified counter-examples. Contrary to Poplack, Clyne (2000: 273), for instance, observes counterexamples to the free-morpheme constraint in his corpus, getting instances of switches between a bound morpheme and a phonologically unintegrated lexical form.

As an additional example, Mahootian (1996: 391) predicts that switches between phonologically unassimilated bound and free morphemes can occur. From her study of Farsi-English CS corpora, which involves language pairs with different basic word orders, she argues that her analysis can account for switches between unassimilated bound and free morphemes.

Ex. 18

Lawyer-*et* will tell you what to do ___-2nd sing___	'Your lawyer will tell you what to do'

Farsi-English., Mahootian (1993b, cited in Mahootian (1996:391)

In the example above, although the Farsi inflectional morpheme {-*et*} is semantically equivalent to *your* in English, the author argues that a code-switched utterance like *et-lawyer* can be found only in the monolingual Farsi utterance *et vaekil*.

3.2.2.2. The equivalence constraint

The second of Poplack's constraint, *the equivalence constrain*, predicts that "CS tends to occur at points in discourse where juxtaposition of two languages does not violate a surface syntactic rule of either language, i.e. at points around which the surface structures of the two languages map on to each other" (Poplack 1980: 586). The general hypothesis is that a code-switch can take place at boundaries common to the grammars of both languages, and switching cannot occur between any two sentence elements unless they are naturally ordered in the same way. Thus, CS from one language to another in the middle of a sentence is only possible if the linear order of the sentences in both languages is preserved. For example, Poplack observes the rare occurrence of Spanish-English switching of the type shown in (19), since the Spanish and English rules for adjective placement are not equivalent.

Ex. 19

| A car *nuevo* | 'A car new' |
| | *'A new car'* |

(Poplack 1980: 586)

These two assumptions have been criticized and questioned. Although Poplack claims that these two constraints on CS are universal, other scholars depending on various corpora representing various types of language contact present counterevidence to these two constraints. For instance, Clyne (2003: 84) referring to his 1987 German and Dutch corpora in Australia, argues that these constraints are not universal and he even regards them as strong tendencies rather than constraints. Moreover, Clyne reformulates Poplack's constraint that the *equivalence constraint* indicates that syntactic overlap facilitates CS not that lack of structural overlap prevents such switching. According to the Facilitation Principle, Clyne (2003: 177) further states, "if syntactic rules overlap between the languages…. switching is facilitated".

Researchers who have analysed switches between languages with different basic word orders, on the other hand, claim that conflicts in CS between differently structured languages cannot be explained in terms of constraints as CS is not only a surface phenomenon. It is argued that CS cannot be explained in terms of surface configurations. Among others, Myers-Scotton (2002: 13) criticizes researchers who suggest constraints on the structure of CS for taking a descriptive approach with their constraints being empirically based, but not motivated by any particular theoretical approach.

3.3. Theoretical model of intrasentential CS

Research on grammatical aspects of CS has focused exclusively on intrasentential CS, so that grammatical theory has primarily focused on relations below the sentence level. It has been argued that only at the intrasentential level researchers are able to observe with some certainty the interaction between two grammatical systems. Aiming at investigating the phenomenon of CS at this level, scholars propose a theoretical model which is called the Matrix Language Model (ML) to account for intra-sentential CS.

3.3.1. The Matrix Language Model (ML)

A number of researchers make some type of distinction between the languages participating in CS. The motivation for the ML hypothesis is the idea that both languages are not equally activated all the time and that the Matrix Language (ML) has a stronger role than the Embedded Language (EL) in a mixed utterance.

The observation of the ML is interpreted differently by researchers as different constituents on CS data and various hypotheses have been proposed to account for intrasentential CS data. As it can be seen in the coming sections of this chapter, researchers differ not only in the criteria they adopt for identifying the Matrix Language, but also with regard to the level at which they assume it should be identified.

3.3.1.1 Early accounts of the Matrix Language Model

3.3.1.1.1. Joshi: Matrix Language Model (ML)

In an early systematic study on intrasentential CS Joshi (1985: 192) referring to her Marathi-English data, formulates a framework to account for intrasentential CS which later on has been called and established as the Matrix Language-Frame Model by other scholars.

Joshi formulates a system in terms of the grammars of the two languages and a switching rule. She tries to show that a variety of observable constraints on intrasentential CS can be formulated in terms of constraints on the switching rule. A distinction is drawn between matrix language (LM) and embedded language (LE) to stand for the languages of a mixed utterance. Matrix language is defined as the language from which the mixed sentence is coming from, and the other language or languages are called the embedded language(s). The model aims to formulate a system characterizing the mixed language (LX). A mixed sentence is one, as she further formulates, containing lexical items from both matrix language and embedded language.

3.3.1.1.1.1. Closed class vs. open class items

Thus the model emphasizes a left-to-right organization in CS and proposes the hypothesis that 'closed-class items' come only from the Matrix Language, which means that switching from category of the Matrix Grammar to a category of the Embedded Language is permitted, but not vice versa. Joshi believes that investigating the relationship between the open and closed class items may give some clues concerning the organization of the grammar and lexicon between the two language systems of intrasentential CS.

However, later research on the grammatical properties of intrasentential CS put great efforts into drawing a distinction between open and closed class items. Lanza (1997: 126), for instance, argues that making a distinction between open class and closed class items is critical and forms the basis for the analysis of the various categories in the mixed utterances. In her terminology, *lexical morphemes* refer to open class items and *grammatical morphemes* refer to closed class items. Open class items, hence, can be distinguished from closed class items in that they include those morphemes that new words or morphemes may be added to. These are nouns, verbs, adverbs and adjectives. Closed class items are pronouns, auxiliaries, modals, determiners, quantifiers, prepositions, tense morphemes, complementizers, etc.

3.3.1.1.1.2. Constraints on closed class items

Regarding the closed class items within the model of ML, Joshi (1985: 193) argues that some categories cannot be switched, and she proposes some constraints on intrasentential CS. For example, she proposes the following constraint:

- Certain closed class items such as tense and auxiliaries cannot be switched when they appear in the main verbal phrase (VP) as illustrated in (20).

Ex. 20

Mula khurcyā *paint* kartāt	'Boys chairs *paint* do+ Tense'
	'The boys *paint*ed the chairs'

Marathi-English, Joshi (1985: 193)

In (20), the root verb *paint*, as Joshi explains, has been switched from English into Marathi, but the closed class item {*tāt*} has not been switched.

Here, it would be interesting and quite important to find out why an open class item is switched, but a closed class item is not. Some researchers try to investigate the correlation between word class and switchability in CS research. Azuma (1997: 117), for instance, proposes that the stand-alone principle, in her terms, can account for such a dichotomy. Open class items are content words which can meaningfully stand alone and thus, as the author argues, can be easily code-switched. Closed class items, on the other hand, are function words which cannot meaningfully stand alone and thus, as she stresses, no CS occurs.

3.3.1.2. Base language vs. embedded language

Some other studies adapting the notion of base language point to the difficulty of determining the directionality of mixing in intrasentential CS on purely structural grounds, and hence the issue of host or base language and embedded language has figured prominently when considering the languages of interaction in intrasentential CS. Appel and Muysken (1987: 121) consider three basic ways to identify the base language, which are psycholinguistic, sociolinguistic and grammatical. Psycholinguistically, they point out that the base language can be thought of as the dominant language of the bilingual speaker making the switch, since that language determines the verbal behaviour of the speaker. Sociolinguistically, the base language is the unmarked linguistic code, while grammatically the base language is the one which imposes a particular constraint for a particular case of switching involved.

3.3.2. Myers-Scotton: Matrix Language Frame Model (MLF)

In general, research on intrasentential CS shows that the bilingual's first language is almost always the language which can be identified as the ML by the morpheme frequency criterion. The Matrix Language Frame Model (MLF) is a constraint-oriented theory, introduced by Myers-Scotton in 1993, developed and expanded in her later publications. This model, as Clyne (2003: 81) argues, is the most comprehensive and influential current framework in language contact studies. The model provides the framework for the identification of the matrix language (ML) and the embedded language (EL). What makes the model so influential, as Lanza (1997: 187) points out, is that the MLF Model does not conceptualize CS as surface-level 'switching'. In presenting the MLF Model, Myers-Scotton (1993: 75) explains that the model is based on the premise that CS takes place within the constraints of a conceptual frame and that the frame is largely set by the semantic and morphosyntactic procedures of only one of the two languages participating in CS.

3.3.2.1. Defining the Matrix Language and the Embedded Language

In her earlier work, Myers-Scotton (1993: 66) argues that both psycholinguistic and sociolinguistic criteria contribute to a definition of the Matrix Language. The sociolinguistic approach is based on the relative frequency of morphemes from the ML and the EL in the interaction type which includes the CS data under study. The psycholoniguistic criterion to be considered in the definition of a Matrix Language is relative proficiency. However, due to the difficulty of measuring linguistic proficiency, as the author argues, this criterion only becomes useful when combined with sociolinguistic data. For example, in those communities which are in the process of language shift, as the immigrant community of this study seems to be, it is especially difficult to identify the speaker's or the childrens' better language.

The model suggests that the participation of the languages involved in intrasentential code-switched utterances is different. Therefore a distinction is made between the Matrix Language and the Embedded Language. The ML can be identified as the language of more morphemes in interaction types including intrasentential CS. Moreover; the Matrix Language is the more dominant language that sets the grammatical frame into which morphemes from another language can be embedded. Hence, ML is described as, "the more dominant language in terms of the number of types of interaction in which it is the more socially unmarked choice" (Myres-Scotton 1993: 67). The Embedded Language, on the other hand, is the less dominant language that participates largely by supplying lexical elements that are integrated into that frame.

In some cases of intrasentential CS, it would be quite problematic to identify the Matrix language and the Embedded Language of a mixed constitute. David and Wei (2004: 4) point to the difficulty of determining the Matrix Language of a code-switched utterance consisting of two words. In doing so, they consider the language that the child is 'supposed' to be speaking with the parent s/he is interacting with, as the Matrix Language.

However, Myres-Scotton in her more recent work modifies some aspects of the MLF Model regarding morpheme frequency and identification of the Matrix Language. Within the terms of the MLF Model, Myres-Scotton (2002: 15) argues that 'contributing more' doesn't mean more morphemes, although this is often the case, but rather contributing more means more abstract structure and structure of a certain type. She (Myres-Scotton 2002: 61) also abandons her previous claim that the Matrix Language can be identified as the source of more morphemes in a discourse sample, for two reasons, as she points out: First, although the language that is the source of the grammatical frame often supplies more morphemes in a mixed constituent, this is not always the case. Second, it is not clear what exactly would constitute a discourse sample.

3.3.2.2. Types of constituents of the MLF Model

The distinction between the ML and the EL in the MLF model allows the model to view intrasentential CS as involved in three types of different but interrelated constituents.

Matrix Language (ML) islands: These are constituents that consist entirely of ML morphemes and in comparison to other languages involved in CS data, ML plays a more dominant role and its grammar sets the morphosyntactic frame for two of the three types of constituents contained in sentences showing intrasentential CS. The ML hypothesis proposes that the ML provides the morphosyntactic frame of ML + EL constituents. Myres-Scotton (2004: 107), in her more recent work, reargues that the role of ML is quite extensive, that it is the source of all syntactic structures of the switched constitute. And the morphosyntactic of ML structures the morphosyntactic frame of the relevant bilingual clause containing CS. Further discussing the crucial role of the ML,

Jake and Myres-Scotton (2009: 212) point out that in CS processes the ML becomes a grammatical construct, they state "when speakers begin to switch, the ML governs grammatical structuring in ways that are largely autonomous from the speaker's intentions that motivate the act of CS in the first place".

ML + EL constituents: These consist of morphemes from both participating languages. The ML + EL is the mixed constituent that contains a single occurring EL lexeme in a frame of any number of ML morphemes. For example, see *a-me-repeat* 'he has repeated' in (21).

Ex. 21

| Mtu *a-me-rpeat* mar any-ingi | 'A person has repeated many times' |

Swahili-English; Myres-Scotton (1988, cited in Myres-Scooton 2002: 57)

The Embedded Language (EL) islands: These constituents are entirely in the embedded language and they are produced when ML morphosyntactic procedures are inhibited and EL procedures are activated. These are well-formed constituents according to the EL grammar. However, the monolingual Embedded Language constituents, in various ways, are controlled by the Matrix Language within the larger bilingual constituent (Myers-Scotton 2002: 25).

3.3.2.3. Content morphemes vs. system morphemes

Another theoretical construct that underlies the MLF Model of intrasentential CS is the content-system morpheme opposition which highlights the importance of recognizing the abstract structure behind surface phrase structures of switched constituents.

Instead of making the distinction between open class and closed class items, Myres-Scotton adopts the terms content and system morphemes to discuss morpheme types in terms of the content vs. system morpheme opposition. The reason for preferring such terms, as Myres-Scotton (2002: 71) explains, is that 'content' is an easily understood term, it also causes few problems as it is semantically more transparent. 'System morpheme' is used because it identifies a class of morphemes more precisely than the other widely used term 'closed class word'.

Thus setting the frame of ML, Myers-Scotton (1993: 6) further makes a division between system and content morphemes. She argues that a morpheme from the other language(s) involved in CS to appear in a ML + EL constituent or in EL islands depends on its status as a system or content morpheme.

It is argued that system morphemes signal relations between morphemes in a sentence and therefore they must come from the Matrix Language. However, it doesn't mean that all system morphemes must come from only one participating language, namely the Matrix Language. To avoid any misunderstanding, Myres-Scotton (2002: 87) further explains the meaning of the *System Morpheme Principle*, stating that only those system morphemes that have grammatical relations external to their head constitute must come from the Matrix Language.

Furthermore, under the notion of quantification, Myers-Scotton (1993: 100) distinguishes system morphemes from content morphemes and argues that any lexical item belonging to a syntactic category which involves quantification is a system morpheme. Hence, system morphemes are quantifiers (e.g. *all, any, no*), affixes, specifiers and inflectional morphology, clitic pronouns, dummy pronouns (*it, there*), possessive adjectives, adverbs expressing intensity or time (*very, soon*), categories expressing person, gender, case and tense. Not all functional words are system morphemes; for example, not all prepositions are system morphemes.

Content morphemes are thematic and their main function will be to express meaning. The content morphemes are verbs, nouns, prepositions, and descriptive adjectives (modifiers), subordinating conjunctions (but, because) and adverbs derived from adjectives. Under the Matrix Language-Embedded Language opposition, while the Embedded Language may supply content morphemes to be inserted into the frame, the Matrix Language is the source of structure for the grammatical frame of the mixed constituents (Myers-Scotton 2002: 20). However, content morphemes can either come from the Matrix Language or the Embedded Language.

3.4. Lexical development of bilingual children

Quite interestingly, the distinction between content and system morphemes has led some researchers to study the development of bilingual children's lexicon in terms of content vs. system morpheme opposition. David and Wei (2004: 1), for instance, using Myers-Scottons' model terms try to investigate the question whether it is possible for a child to develop system and content morphemes separately in two languages, i.e. can a bilingual child have one type of morphemes in one language and another type of morphemes in the other language, or does the child have both types of morphemes in one language and only one type of morphemes in the second one?

In a conclusion of their larger study which was conducted on a group of bilingual children in England, all between the age of 16 and 30 months, David and Wei (2004: 11) found out that no child had only content morphemes in one language and system morphemes in the other, and that a bilingual child seemed to be unable to develop only system morphemes in one language.

However, in a case where the child would have both types of morphemes in one language but only one type in the other, the two authors further propose that the language with both system and content morphemes would be the Matrix Language and would be the one laying the constraints.

4. Functional factors on CS

Most of what has been discussed so far on CS has been based on a mainly linguistic perspective; namely, how linguistic characteristics of involved languages constraint CS when speakers code-switch. This chapter attempts to address some of the social and psychological factors that involve and influence the occurrence of CS. It is strongly argued that CS between languages is not only constrained by linguistic factors, but that the choice of codes is narrowly constrained by social norms as well.

It is argued that the speaker's pragmatic competence enables bilinguals to determine the choice of one language over the other in a particular interaction. Studies show that bilinguals make their language choice on the basis of a number of factors such as with whom, about what, and when and where a speech act occurs. For example, Ritchie and Bhatia (2004: 339) point to four factors that determine language choice and mixing on the part of bilinguals:

(1) The social roles and relationships of the participants

(2) Situational factors: discourse topic and language allocation

(3) Message-intrinsic considerations.

(4) Language attitudes including social dominance and security.

4.1. Situational vs. metaphorical switching

An early approach to stress the functional aspects of CS has been a case study conducted in rural Norway by Bloom and Gumperz. Their main emphasis remains on the concepts of setting, social situation, and social event to explain CS. In their study, Bloom and Gumperz (1972: 424) distinguish between situational and metaphorical CS. The notion of situational switching, as the authors point out, assumes a direct relationship between language and social situation. The term situational switching implies that CS is ruled by components of the speech event, such as topic and participants. The data from their study, as an example, shows that greetings and inquiries about family members tend to be exchanged in the local dialect, while the business part of the transaction is carried out in standard Norwegian.

This approach has been criticized by some researchers. Myers-Scotton (1993: 115), for instance, emphasizes that in this kind of switching it is still the speaker who has the choice to respond to the change in the social setting. Merys-Scotton stresses that in situational CS the change in codes is motivated by the speaker and not driven by the situation. In situational CS, it remains up to the speaker to make the choice to act upon the situational factors of any kind. Situational CS, in general, is determined by factors outside the content of the particular interaction. Differences in status between groups of speakers of languages are some of these factors.

The term metaphorical CS, on the other hand, refers to the communicative effect a speaker wants to convey through CS. The code-switch relates to particular kinds of topics or subject matters rather than to change in social situation.

4.2. 'We code' vs. 'they code' opposition

In his more recent work, Gumperz (1982: 66) introduces the concepts of 'we code' and 'they code' to make a symbolic distinction between the ethnic language of a bilingual community and the language of the wider society within which that community forms a minority. The opposition of 'we code' and 'they code' thus presupposes a particular relationship between the ethnic community and the society at large and within the minority group itself:

> The tendency is for the ethnically specific, minority language to be regarded as the 'we code' and become associated with in-group and informal activities, and for the majority language to serve as the 'they code' associated with the more formal, stiffer and less personal out-group relations.
> (Gumperz 1982: 66)

The concepts of 'we code' and 'they code' have been used by many researchers and for most of them, these terms refer to the ethnic language of a bilingual community and the language of the mainstream society. Jørgensen (1998: 237), for instance, makes use of the 'we code' and 'they code' concepts in accounts of CS behaviour and argues that for linguistic minorities, the difference in status between languages is indeed an important factor. The author points out that in the case of minorities, the 'we code' relates to low prestige where its use is restricted to private spheres, and at the same time a sign of belonging to the minority. The author draws on his previous longitudinal study of the bilingual development of Turkish-speaking children in Danish schools. The code-switches of the study show that Danish works as a 'they code' and Turkish as a 'we code'. The author (Jørgensen 1998: 247) points to a conversation from the study in which Danish is used for the 'public' content, while Turkish is used for private business and for emotional utterances. In this way, the author emphasises that the division of labour between the languages reflects the overall relationship between Danish and Turkish in the everyday lives of these children.

In a similar study on Panjabi-English CS of the bilingual speakers of Panjabi ethnic community in Briton, Romaine (1994: 61) gives examples in which Panjabi serves to mark the in-group of Panjabi-English bilinguals and English the out-group as illustrated in (22).

Ex. 22

| Grezi sikhi e te *why can't they learn*? | 'I learn English, so *why can't they learn* [Asian languages]?' |

Romaine (1994: 61)

Here the switch from Panjabi to English, as the author argues, emphasizes the boundaries between 'them' and 'us'.

4.3. The Markedness model

Markedness model is a theoretical model which has been proposed by Myers-Scotton to provide a general theoretical explanation of the sociolinguistic and pragmatic aspects of CS. The markedness model takes both the social motivations and the psychological forces into consideration that underlie CS. Myers-Scotton (1988:178) distinguishes between unmarked and marked language choice. The explanation of the model emphasizes linguistic choices as negotiations of personal rights and obligations relative to those of other participants in a talk exchange. The basic theoretical assumptions of the model are that, according to Myers-Scotton, interaction types in every conversational situation are conventionalized and have relatively fixed schemata about the role relations between speakers. The unmarked choice depends on a "rights and obligations set associated with a particular conventionalized exchange" whereas the marked choice signals that "the speaker is trying to negotiate a different rights and obligations balance".

The markedness model emphasizes that the participants know which languages are the unmarked and marked choices in a community based on a common, shared experience and that speakers make rational choices intending to achieve the best outcome for them. For the speaker, Myers-Scotton (1988: 156) argues, CS is a tool, a means of doing something by affecting the rights and obligations balance. In her later work, Myers-Scotton (1993: 108) states, "speakers know at an unconscious level that certain choices are unmarked affirmations of the expected and others implicate 'something else' is clear from that conscious remarks they sometimes make about linguistic choices". Hence, the author stresses that explaining a speaker's code selections is successful only if the analyst begins by assuming that speakers are rational actors.

A speaker, thus, may comply with the unmarked rights and obligations sets on the basis of non-linguistic conditions, such as his/her identity, degree of formality; or s/he may wish to establish a new RO set by using a marked one to maintain or change the relations in an interaction. In CS, when the speaker uses the unexpected code to achieve a strategic effect in conversation, this phenomenon is called 'CS as a marked choice'. If, however, the speaker confirms to the expected code to maintain a desired situation or meaning, this is called 'CS as an unmarked choice'. Myers-Scotton (1995: 119) points out that some certain conditions must be met for the occurrence of unmarked CS; such switching typically does not happen when there is a socio-economic difference between speakers or when they are strangers. However, proficiency in the languages is not a sufficient condition. Unmarked CS will be informal and involve only in-group members.

5. Speech community

5.1. Use of the term

Sociolinguistic studies point out that it is not possible to use the term 'speech community' without much difficulty, a term which probably derived from the German *Sprachgemeischaft*. In sociolinguistics, as Patrick (2002: 574) stresses, there is remarkably little agreement on the use of the term- speech community. For example, the term has been used for both large and small geographically bounded urban communities; for minority groups; for urban immigrants, as distinct from both their source and target groups. However, cutting across geographic lines, the term has been used to refer to very general assemblages such as children.

In early studies, the term has been used to refer to people who use the same speech signals and thereby emphasize large-scale groups that share a language. In this way, Chomsky (1965: 3) for instance, describes the ideal speaker in the ideal speech community, and proposes the notion of a completely homogeneous speech community. In contrary to this approach, Wardhaugh (1986: 121) emphasizes that the concept of speech community must be flexible and that choosing a group to be identified with the term speech community should change according to situation. The author explains the case of an immigrant community member who lives in a bilingual setting. In such a case, a bilingual speaker from the community may switch her/his speech from one speech community to another, possibly even in the course of a single utterance. Thus, s/he may belong to one speech community at one moment and to a different one at another. More broadly, Montgomery (1986: 201) argues that as an idealized notion, the term can be referred to a group that shares speech characteristics such as a language in common; common ways of using language; common reactions and attitudes to language; and common social bonds.

5.2. Definitions of speech community

As the previous discussion has shown the term speech community is widely used by sociolinguists to refer to a community based on language. However, there has been considerable confusion and disagreement over what a speech community exactly is. While some scholars define speech communities by their linguistic characteristics, others insist that using linguistic elements alone to determine what is or is not a speech community has proven to be quite impossible because, as it is argued, there is not such a strong relationship between linguistic characteristics and speech community. For instance, Bloomfield (1933: 42) emphasizes the concept of communication and describes the linguistic distribution within a social or geographical space in terms of speech community. He defines speech community as, "a group of people who interact by means of speech". More broadly the term speech community has been described as the language spoken in the bilingual's neighbourhood, his ethnic group, his church group, his occupation group, and his recreation group. However, for general linguistics, speech community has been described as all the people who speak a single language and so share notions of what is same or different in phonology or grammar.

Other sociolinguists find no reasons or a priori grounds that force them to define speech communities as all members of the community are supposed to speak the same language. For instance, Gumperz (1968: 463) employs the term linguistic community and offers a different definition of that term as, "a social group which may be either monolingual or multilingual held together by frequency of social interaction patterns and set of from the surrounding areas by weakness in the lines of communication". Thus, it is not supposed for all the members of the same speech community to speak the same language or use the same linguistic forms on similar occasions. "All that is required", a later definition by Gumperz (1986: 16) states, "is that there is at least one language in common and that rules governing basic communicative strategies be shared so that speakers can decode the social meanings carried by alternative modes of communication". However, Gumperz (2001: 43) insists that linguistic phenomena are analysable both within the context of language itself and within the broader context of social behaviour. The universe of speech community, as the author further argues, refers to the analysis of linguistic phenomena within a socially defined universe.

Labov (1972; cited in Wardhaugh 1986: 115), puts emphasis on the non-linguistic characteristics and the social norms of the community that make individuals feel that they are members of the same community. Labov states that "speech community is not defined by any marked agreement in the use of language elements, so much as by participation in a set of shared norms; these norms may be observed in overt types of evaluative behaviour, and by the uniformity of abstract patterns of variation which are invariant in respect to particular levels of usage". Similarly, Romaine (1994: 22) emphasizes that the boundaries between speech communities are essentially social rather than linguistic.

She refers to speech community as a group of people who do not necessarily share the same language, but share a set of norms and rules for the use of language.

6. The Study

This chapter shall introduce the case study of this book. First of all the fieldwork and the community will be presented; then, the two languages discussed here, Kurdish and German will be presented. The focus will be on the Kurdish language; an introduction to selected linguistic features of Kurdish in comparison to German will be discussed, specifically those linguistic aspects which are of certain importance in dealing with Kurdish-German CS data of the study.

6.1. The fieldwork: Kurdish immigrant community

The data source of this study is the Kurdish immigrant community in Austria. First of all it is necessary to make a socio-political remark regarding the origins and backgrounds of the immigrant community the study is based on.

The subjects of this study are pre-school Kurdish-German bilingual children from the Iraqi members of the Kurdish immigrant community in Austria. In general, the community has other members of the Republic of Turkey, Iran and Syria, where Kurds live. However, the origins of the members of the ethnic community of this study go back to Iraq. In Iraq the term "Kurdistan" is widely used to refer to the Kurdish area of northern Iraq, where Kurds predominate. After the fall of Saddam Hussein in 2003 the region was recognized as the Kurdistan Region of Iraq by the new Iraqi constitution (Article 113, New Iraqi Constitution 2005).

The members of the community are somehow newcomers in Austria. Recently, at the beginning of the 1990s and after the first Gulf War against Iraq, early members of the community- namely the first generation arrived or fled to Austria as asylum seekers. Thus the community had its beginnings in the middle of the 1990s. After some years under really hard conditions as asylum seekers, they became political refugees and since then have started to settle their lives in Austria. Family reunification, the arrival of new asylum seekers, marriage and giving birth to children are the main sources of new members in the community and ultimately the community is ever growing. However, compared to other ethnic communities, e.g. the Turkish community, the Kurdish community in Austria is rather small. In Austria, Kurds are a minority among the immigrants. However, it is difficult to give statistics, showing the number of immigrant Kurds in Austria and in Europe in general. Since Kurds do not have an independent state and live in the four mentioned countries, statistic makes on Kurdish immigrants in Europe are included in the statistics on Iraqis, Turks, Syrians, and Iranians. As Backus (2004: 690) states "it is difficult to say how great the proportion of Kurds is among the [Turkish] immigrants, with estimates sometimes ranging up to 30 percent".

It should be kept in mind that this study is conducted on the Iraqi Kurds of the community only- as the Kurdish community in Austria has more members of Kurds from the Republic of Turkey. But since the Kurds from Turkey have very different political, social and linguistic backgrounds, they have not been included in the study.

6.1.1. An asylum community

The Kurdish community in Austria and all over Europe has not yet become an established immigrant community. The case of the Kurdish community in Europe differs from other immigrant communities in a crucial way, especially for the first generation of the community. Almost all members of the first generation of the community arrived Austria as asylum seekers and not as immigrants or workers, consequently this fact gives the community the status of an asylum community rather than an immigrant community. The Kurdish term '*komalgai tarauga*' which means something like 'exiled community' or 'sheltered community' gives special political, social and linguistic status to the members of the community as compared to most of immigrant communities in Austria.

Their conditions in Austria as asylum seekers simply indicate that their departure from their homeland is not encouraged by the Iraqi state, and on the other hand their arrival to Austria is not definitely accepted by the Austrian authorities. For asylum seekers it takes years or a decade in some cases to get asylum rights and become political refugees and finally to adopt citizenship of the host country. Thus problems of discrimination, alienation, and the breaking down of family structures plague the first generation. Integration problems are an almost inevitable result of the uprooting associated with their condition as asylum seekers.

As far as the second generation of the community is concerned, namely the Austrian-born or Austrian-raised children of the community, this generation has not yet come of age and is not well established. These members are still very young; the majority of them are young children and others have not yet passed their teenage stage. The majority of the members of the second generation have never been to their homeland- the Kurdistan Region of Iraq. And the reason is obvious; their parents, namely the first generation of the community, are asylum seekers or political refugees (at the best condition), therefore going back home to Iraq even for a short visit is regarded illegal by both Austrian and Iraqi authorities.

6.1.2. The Kurdish speech community

Kurdish is the mother tongue of the Kurdish speech community. The Kurdish language (Kurdî or كوردى) is a term used for the language spoken by Kurds. The Kurdish language belongs to the north western sub-group of the Iranian languages, which themselves belong to the Indo-Iranian branch of the Indo-European language family. Kurdish is therefore almost as different from Turkish and Arabic as English and French, but very similar to Farsi, the national language of Iran (Kreyenbroek 1992: 70). The Kurdish language ranks fortieth in the world in terms of the number of speakers, 25 to 30 million (Hassanpour 2000: 33). It is mainly spoken in parts of Iran, Iraq, Syria, and Turkey. In Iraq 'the Arabic and the Kurdish language are the two official languages' (Article 4, Iraqi New Constitution 2005).

Hamasaeed (1999: 15) distinguishes two main dialect groups of Kurdish, namely North Kurmanji and South Kurmanji. This study is based on data taken from Sorani sub-dialect of South Kurmanji speakers of Kurdish. So the data of this study is based on Sorani Kurdish, which is also called Sulaimaniya Kurdish. Of all the Kurdish dialects in Iraq, that of Sulaimaniya seems to enjoy the greatest cultural prestige, as is acknowledged by speakers of other dialects. It is the Sulamaniya dialect that the central government in Baghdad has chosen to be used in Kurdish textbooks for elementary schools throughout Iraqi Kurdistan (McCarus 1958: 10). As Hamasaeed (1999: 17) points out, the Sulaimaniya dialect is regarded as the standard language of almost all Kurds in Iraq and Iran.

In all those states where Kurds live the Kurdish language has been subject to harsh measures of suppression. As a result, as Hassanpour (2000: 33) states, "An integral part element of this policy has been the suppression of academic study of the language, its dialects, geography, and history. Even in Iraq, where the language was tolerated as an official language, a policy of Arabization was practised as a means of containing Kurdish nationalism". That is why academic studies on the Kurdish language can hardly be found in the literature.

6.2. The languages of this study

Since this study is on Kurdish-German CS, it is important to provide an introduction to selected linguistic aspects of Kurdish in comparison to German, specifically those aspects which are of certain importance in dealing with Kurdish-German CS phenomena in the collected data. In order to make those linguistic features of Kurdish more explicit, they will be compared to English as well. Most information about the Kurdish grammar was taken from McCarus (1958) and Hamasaeed (1999), who both analyse Sulaimanyia Kurdish in their work.

In the following sections some linguistic aspects of the Kurdish language such as inflectional morpheme, phrasal structure, pro-drop parameter and gender distinction will be briefly explained and compared to German language. Examples will be given from Kurdish language; the examples will be classified according to their Kurdish internal linguistic constituency and for each example its glossing and then its translation into English will be provided.

6.2.1. Inflectional morphemes

Kurdish has a rich inflectional morphology and this aspect of Kurdish plays an important role in Kurdish-German CS. For that reason, a detailed description will be given on the patterning and meaning of the inflectional morphemes for some selected word classes of Kurdish such as *noun*, *pronoun* and *verb*. As Fox (1990: 104) points out, German also makes extensive use of inflections that involve the indication of certain grammatical categories. In both Kurdish and German two types of inflections can be distinguished; *declension*, which applies to nouns, pronouns, and *conjugation* which applies to verbs.

6.2.1.1. Noun inflection / Declension

6.2.1.1.1. Noun inflection in Kurdish

A Kurdish noun in the absolute state, i.e. without any ending of any kind, gives a generic sense of the noun. It is also the "lexical" form of the noun.

6.2.1.1.1.1. Definition

In the Kurdish language, nouns are words which take definition and number suffixes. So, in Kurdish nouns can be inflected for definition and number.

Definite suffix:

The noun is represented by the uninflected word stem {0}. In general, the noun shows inflection for definition or lack of definition. A singular noun is made definite ('the') by attaching suffixes to it. The usual definite suffix is {-aka} after consonants and {-ka} after vowels affixed directly to the noun stem that precedes all other suffixes in order of suffixation as the example in (23) illustrates.

Ex. 23

Kurdish realization	Glossing	Translation
Kic N + {0}	'Girl'	
Kic-aka N + df.	'Girl-df.'	'*The girl*'

In (23), which shows an example from Kurdish, the definite morpheme {-aka} appears after the noun 'Kic' _ '*Girl*', and it behaves as a suffix but it functions as an article, that has been affixed directly to the noun stem.

Indefinite suffix:

The sign of indefinite singular (a, any, some) is the indefinite suffix {-ek} after consonants and {-yek} after vowels, affixed directly to the noun stem, as illustrated in (24).

Ex. 24

Pyaw N + {0}	'*Man*'	
Pyaw-ek N + indf.	'Man-a'	'*A man*'

McCarus (1958: 48)

So in Kurdish instead of articles inflections are used and suffixed directly to the noun stem.

But in German as well as in English an article comes before the noun and no morpheme affixed to the noun stem as illustrated in (25).

Ex. 25

| Das Mädchen | *'The girl'* |
| df. artic. + N | |

6.2.1.1.1.2. Number

In the Kurdish language, nouns are inflected for singular and plural. The singular is represented by the uninflected word stem {0}; for the great majority of nouns the plural is formed by the suffixation of {-an} after constants and {-kan} after vowels as in (26).

Ex. 26

Taxta	*'Board'*
N + {0}	
Taxta-kan	*'Boards'*
N + pl.	

McCarus (1958: 48)

6.2.1.1.2. Personal pronoun inflection

6.2.1.1.2.1. Personal pronouns

Kurdish pronouns show distinction of person and number. Syntactically, they differ from nouns in that nouns occur in agreement with verbs only in the third person, whereas pronouns occur in agreement with verbs in the first and second persons as well.

Person: Pronouns show first, second, and third person. These forms are all suppletive, and are listed below.

Number: Pronouns show two numbers, singular and plural. The plurals in the first and second person are suppletive, only in the third person is the plural derived from the singular by the affixation of {-*an*}. The pronouns are listed below:

	Singular		Plural	
1st person	Min	'*I, me*'	Ema	'*we, us*'
2nd person	To	'*you*-sg.'	Ewa	'*you*-pl.'
3rd person	Aw	'*he, she, her, it*'	Awan	'*they*'

McCarus (1958: 51)

The personal pronouns are used as possesors when occurred after the possesive morpheme {-i} as illustrated in (27).

Ex. 27

Ktawaka-i mn	Book-poss. I
N + Poss. Pers. Pron.	'*My book*'

6.2.1.1.3. Nouns with pronominal suffixes

The pronominal suffixes are suffixes which can be attched to nouns without converting them to a different word class. The pronominal suffixes express both person and number, they are listed as below:

	Singular	Plural
1st person	{-*m*}	{-*man*}
2nd person	{-*t*}	{-*tan*}
3rd person	{-*i*}	{-*yan*}

McCarus (1958: 46)

These pronominal suffixes added to nouns have the meaning of possessor as illustrated in (28).

Ex. 28

Naw	'Name'
N + {0}	
Naw-m	'Name-poss.'
N + poss. sg.	'*My name*'

McCarus (1958: 49)

In (28) the pronominal inflectional morpheme {-*m*} has been affixed directly to the noun stem "Naw". It adds the meaning of possessor to the noun stem.

6.2.1.1.2. Noun Inflection in German

In German, the inflection for nouns, adjectives, pronouns, and articles indicates grammatical categories such as number and gender (masculine, feminine, neuter), and case (nominative, genitive, dative, and accusative), as shown in (29).

Ex. 29

Der gute Mann	'*The good man*'
Den guten Mann	'*The good man*'
Des guten Mannes	'*The good man*'
Dem guten Mann	'*The good man*'

Fox (1990: 113)

6.2.1.2. Verb inflection / conjugation

6.2.1.2.1. Verb inflection in Kurdish

In the Kurdish language verbs must show the following main categories by means of formal features:

- Person (1st, 2nd, 3rd) and number (singular and plural)
- Tense
- Mood (indicative, subjunctive, imperative)

Person and number: In the Kurdish language person and number are indicated by means of suffixation in all tenses except the imperfect. Two sets of suffixes are used, one for transitive verbs in the past tenses, and another for all other verbs. Transitive verbs in the past tenses indicate person and number by the pronominal suffixes (see 6.2.1.1.3.), whereas intransitive verbs in the past tenses and all verbs, both transitive and intransitive, in the present tenses indicate person and number by the verbal suffixes below, which are similar to the English present-tense copula (*am, is, are*).

	Singular	Plural
1st person	C{-*im*}, V{-*m*}	C{-in}, V{-n}
2nd person	C{-i (t)}, V{-y (t)}	C{-in}, V{-n}
3rd person	C{-e (t) }, V{-a (t)}	C{-in}, V{-n}

McCarus (1958: 52)

In the above table the {(-*t*)} of the 2nd and 3rd singular is omissible, without difference in meaning. The abbreviations ''C-'' and ''V-'' mean after constant and after vowel.

6.2.1.2.2. Verb inflection in German

In German, the verb takes a large number of different forms that reflects the different grammatical categories involved. Thus verb inflection may indicate number (singular or plural), person (1st, 2nd, and 3rd), tense (present, past), mood (indicative, subjunctive), voice (active, passive), infinitive, etc., as shown in (30).

Ex. 30

Ich trage	Es trägt
Du trägst	Wir tragen
Er trägt	Ihr tragt
Sie trägt	Sie tragen

(Fox 1990: 103)

The structure of verbal forms in (30) consists of a verb-stem with a suffix indicating the grammatical categories mentioned above. German, as noted by (Haider 2010: 272), has three categories of non-finite verb forms that combine with other verbs. The morphological construction of these verb forms are shown and exemplified as following.

Bare infinitive form: The infinitive form is characterised by the suffix {-en}, as illustrated in (31a).

Infinitive with a prefixed particle *zu*: This from is a cognate of English 'to' plus the infinitve form, as shown in (31b).

Past participle form: The past participle form, except for the irregular verbs, is prefixed with {*ge*-}, and suffixed with {-t}, as in (31d).

Ex. 31

a) suchen	'*seek*'
b) zu suchen	'*to seek*'
c) gesucht	'*sought*'

(Haider 2010: 272)

In German, as (Haider 2010: 273) further notes, {*zu*} is a morphological part of each verb and it has the properties of an affix, just like the participle prefix {ge-}. Whereas, in English the participle 'to' is categorized as an independent functional head element rather than an inflectional particle prefixed to the verb.

6.2.2. Negation

In Kurdish, all verbs are negated merely by prefixing the verbs with '*not*'. The main negative prefix is {*na-*}, its basic meaning are denying the realization of the action or state denoted by the verb. Examples are shown in (32).

Ex. 32

| Mn axom | '*I eat*' |
| Mn na-xom | 'I not-eat' '*I don't eat*' |

McCarus (1958: 69)

6.2.3. Phrasal structure in Kurdish

In Kurdish, phrases consist of a single head and its modifiers. They are of two types, nominal and verbal.

6.2.3.1. Nominal phrases

The head of the nominal phrase may be a noun, an adjective, a pronoun, or a particle. The modifiers are of two classes: Those which follow the head and are linked to it by the inflectional morpheme {-i}, e.g. including nouns, adjectives, and pronouns. And those which precede the head but are not formally linked to it, these are called pre-head modifiers. The traditional term for the {-i} inflectional morpheme is *izafa*, which is taken from the Arabic grammar. The most common type of nominal phrase consists of head, *izafa*, and modifier, which can be diagrammed as *Head + i + modifier*.

However, the *izafa* morpheme has also been called possessive morpheme (Hamasaeed 1999: 42), as it links the two parts of a possessive construction and is equivalent to the English '*of*', as illustrated in (33).

Ex. 33

Sar-i to	'Head-of you'
N + Poss. Pron.	'*Your head*'

(Hamasaeed 1999:43)

6.2.3.2. Verbal phrase

This is a construction that minimally consists of a head and its modifier. The head is a verb and the modifier may be an adverb, a noun, or an adjective. The modifier precedes the verb, as shown in (34).

Ex. 34

Sag-aka lera darka	'Dog-the here take-out'
Subj. + df. Adv. V	'*Take the dog out of here*'

McCarus (1958: 95)

6.2.3.2.1. Verbal phrases with the Kurdish operator *krdn*

Kurdish verbal phrases may consist of an operator in combination with a major category such as noun, adjective or verb. These verbal phrases are very common in the Kurdish language and any noun or adjective can potentially occur with an operator in a verbal phrase. The most common operators that occur in combination with a noun, a verb or an adjective are '*krdn*' which means '*to do*' or '*make*' and '*bu*' meaning '*to become*' (McCarus 1958: 104). As illustrated in (35).

Ex. 35

Bang-krdn	'Call-to do'
N + op.	'*To call*'
Pak-krd	'Clean-do'
Adj. + op.	'*To clean*'

McCarus (1958: 95)

The verbs *krdn* _'*do*' and *bu* _'*to become*' have been categorized as light verbs. Haig (2007: 174), for instance, points out that in the Kurdish language new verbs are created by combining a non-verbal element such as noun, adjective, adverb or even a sort of phrase with the so called light verbs *krdn* or *bu*, and the resulting expressions are compound-like units that behave like a simple verb form. The author argues that due to the luck of productive morphological derivation of new verbs in Kurdish, the *krdn* construction is used as a strategy to create new verbs or to incorporate borrowed lexical items, such as nouns, verbs or anything else in the donor language, as shown in (36).

Ex. 36

| Fehm-krdn | 'Understanding-do' |
| V + op. | '*To understand*' |

Haig (2007: 174)

In (36) the verbal noun *fehm* is a borrowed lexical item from Arabic into Kurdish. As Haig explains, the Arabic verbal noun *fehm* is incorporated into Kurdish by combining it with the Kurdish operator *krdn*.

It is very common that inflectional morpheme(s) may occur between the operator and the major category, as shown in (37).

Ex. 37

Nasriin paak-i-krd-nawa	'Nasriin clean-them-done-has'
N adj. +2nd sg. + op. + tense	*'Nasriin has cleaned them'*

(Hamasaeed 1999: 122)

6.2.3.3. Prepositional phrase

Prepositions occur only with nominal phrases, preceding the head of the noun. Only two prepositions show morphemic alternates which are {*la*} '*in, at, from, by*' and {*ba*} '*in, at*' and {*pe*} 'to'. The morpheme {*la*} occurs with pronominal suffixes. The preposition itself marks the beginning of the prepositional phrase, and the end of the complement is marked by a postpositional element like {-*awa*} or {*da*}. This is illustrated in (38).

Ex. 38

La bakh-aka-da	'In garden-the-prep.'
Prep. N-df. sg.-prep.	*'In the garden'*

(Hamasaeed1999: 102)

The morphological construction of phrases in German will be discussed in the following section.

6.2.4. Clause word order

The word order in Kurdish is basically different from English but similar to German. In terms of OV vs. VO categorization, Kurdish and German are classified as OV languages, whereas English is classified as VO.

Kurdish is a verb final language and has a Subject Object Verb (SOV) word order. As has already been mentioned, Kurdish has a rich inflectional morphology. As far as Kurdish word order is concerned, the inflected element on the verb has been regarded as a constituent in the clause word order of Kurdish. Ha-

masaeed (1999: 106), for instance, proposes the following word order for Kurdish:
- S O V I

The inflected verb always occurs at the end of the clause, as illustrated in (39).

Ex. 39

| Asad Aram dagr-et | 'Asad Aram caches' |
| N.   N.   V. + Subj. Infl. | *'Asad caches Aram'* |

Hamasaeed (1999: 106)

German, however, is not a 'strict' OV language. Strict OV languages are described as languages in which any phrasal head is a phrase-final one. Haider (2010: 130) points out that in German head-final phrases has the property of word order variation, whereas, head-initial phrases such as noun phrases are ordered strictly. As Haider (2010: 5) states, "German is OV only in the literal reading, insofar as this refers to the structure of the verb phrase: the verb as the head of the VP [verbal phrase] follows its nominal complements", as illustrated in (40).

Ex. 40

Jemandem etwas *fragen*	'Someone something *ask*'
	'Ask someone something'

Haider (2010: 6)

In English which is a 'strict' VO language, the verb precedes its nominal complements, as illustrated in (41).

Ex. 41

Ask someone something

6.2.5. Other phenomena

6.2.5.1. Pro-drop / Null-subject parameter

In linguistic typology, a null subject [+ pro-drop] language, like Italian, Spanish, or Persian refers to a language whose grammar permits an independent clause to lack an explicit subject, i.e., its main characteristic is that subject pronouns can be omitted. Such a clause is then said to have a null subject. Typically, null subject languages express person, number, or gender agreement with the referent on the verb, rendering a subject noun phrase redundant.

The two languages, namely German and Kurdish analysed in this study differ with respect to the analysis of null-subjects. Kurdish is a pro drop language, i.e. it allows the omission of subject pronouns. In Kurdish the subject may be expressed within the verb by the person-number suffix (the implicit subject), thus a verb may constitute a complete clause as itself. The following types of clauses may occur:

- S O V

Ex. 42

Xawanmał kaxaz-aka axwene	'The host letter-the reads'
Sub. Obj. V	*'The host reads the letter'*

McCarus (1958: 98)

- V

Ex. 43

Hat	'Came'
V	'*(S/he) come*'

McCarus (1958: 97)

In (43), the subject pronoun (s/he) has been omitted.

German, as well as English, are non Null-subject [- pro-drop] languages; they acquire an explicit subject. German, however, as Kaltenbacher (2001: 71) points out allows null-subjects under specific conditions, namely if only the subjects appear in sentence initial position in main declarative clauses, as illustrated in (44).

Ex. 44

| Question: Seit wann bist du schon hier? | *'Since when have you been here?'* |
| Response: Bin eben erst nach hause gekommen. | *'Just arrived home.'* |

Kaltenbacher (2001: 71)

6.2.5.2. Case morphology

Kurdish and German nouns differ in case morphology. For example, English and German noun phrases have the following different case forms:

Nominative: English; I, you, he, she, it
German; Ich, du, er, sie, es
Accusative: English; me, you, him, her, it
German; mich, dich, ihn, sie, es
Genitive: English; ---
German; meine, deine, seine, ihre
Dative: English; him, her, it
German; mir, ihm, ihr

(Hamasaeed 1999: 125)

But Kurdish, as Hamasaeed (1999: 125) points out, has none of these case forms. For example '*I*' and '*me*' are the same, as are '*he*' and '*him*', '*she*' and '*her*'.

6.2.5.3. Gender distinction

The Sorani dialect of Kurdish has no grammatical gender. There are no pronouns to distinguish between masculine and feminine and no verb inflection to signal gender. German, for instance, has articles inflected for gender, such as *der*, *die* and *das*, but Kurdish has none of them. Even for the subject pronouns, such as *him, her* and *it* in English, Kurdish has no gender distinctions. The subject pronouns and their gender type can be identified with the inflectional morpheme on the verb or within the context of the utterance.

7. Subjects and recordings

This chapter introduces the subjects and the data the present study is based on. The presentation of the subjects includes a description of their family background as well as the contact to the languages they acquire. Furthermore, the procedure for data collection and methodology, for example how the data have been collected, and the description of speech situations are outlined. This information is necessary for a precise analysis of language choice and language mixing.

In chapter 8, the data will be introduced. The detailed presentation of the data will introduce only the code-switches that occurred in the data and the monolingual conversations that are exclusively Kurdish or German produced by the subjects will be excluded. All code-switches will be extracted for analysis. The data will then be observed (in chapter 9) to support or refuse the predictions for intrasentential CS mentioned in the theoretical part of this book and also (in chapter 10) to analyse the data according to social factors on CS.

7.1. Method of observation

The type of observation which was applied is tape recording of spontaneous speech. However the method of participant-observation was also used when it was needed. The tape-recordings took place in a very spontaneous atmosphere. The data have been collected in different speech situations such as in the family home during daily interaction, in the playgrounds, and in the community's collective celebrations such as family parties. The aim was to get examples of CS in as many different conversation situations as possible.

In order to get valid and most natural data, or in other words so as to overcome *Labov's paradox* that the observer has to observe how people speak when they are not being observed (Labov 1972: 113), the children were not given special topics to talk about or create any artificial speech situation. Furthermore as a member of the community I had the chance to build up confidence and a certain social binding with the families and especially with their young children, who are the subjects of the study. This was important so as to make the children get accustomed to my presence, so that they did not feel uncomfortable and thus produce less output or less natural data.

In all settings of observation, two subjects of the participants had two very small digital audio-receivers (tape-recorders) with them, which had been fixed to their jackets or put into their pockets. The size of the tape-recorders did not cause any kind of disturbance or difficulty for the subjects and let them to forget about the recording process very soon because the children could move quite freely and could even run around as the tape-recorders were still recording.

As far as the parents are concerned, it seemed that for most of the parents it was of great importance and considerable interest that the speech of their children formed the focus of a project on Kurdish-German bilingualism: Parents often worry about the linguistic development of their children and for them language mixing by the children is an indicator of lack of ability to use the two languages, especially the home language.

7.2. Subjects

As has been mentioned, data are drawn from young Kurdish-German bilingual children. The only particular criterion which was relevant for choosing the participants was age; all the target-subjects of this study are pre-school bilingual children, aged 2 to 6. The children are all born and raised in Austria by Kurdish parents, which means that they have Kurdish as their mother tongue (speech community, L1) and German as their second language (national language, L2). Thus the parents share the same native language, which is Kurdish, but the dominant language of the society at large is German. All of these children, when they are about three years old, start to learn German in a German kindergarten or from their German speaking playmates.

As far as parents-children discourse is concerned it could be observed that the parents' strategy was to keep speaking their home language to their children, mostly trying to reinforce Kurdish as the family language.

7.3. Recordings

Table 1 gives information about the recordings including date and time, participants and speech situations of each recording. All the participants whose speech was recorded and then transcribed are included, but the target-subjects are the pre-school children.

Table 1: Speech situations of the recordings

Time of recordings	Participants	Speech situations
First rec. 23.02.2010 130 minutes	Father: worker Mother: house wife Child 1: male, 2;8 Child 2: female, 4;6, attends kindergarten	In the house of the first family in Vienna. The children interact with their parents and sometimes with the observer and a friend of both the observer and the family.
Second rec. 25.02.2010 180 minutes	Father: driver Mother: house wife Child1: female, 2;7 Child2: female, 4;2, attends kindergarten Two adults: over 12 years old	In the house of the second family. The two children interact with their parents and their elder sisters.
Third rec. 27.02.2010 100 minutes	Father: student at Vienna University Mother: house wife Child1: male, 5;8, attends kindergarten Child2: male, 2-3 years old Child3: male, 4-5 years old	In a party where a lot of the families of the community are present. Child 1 carries a small digital audio-receiver in his pocket. He is always with three of his friends who are also of pre-school age. They play and run around; sometimes they interact with some adults of the community. Due to the loud music of the party, the recorded speech is not always clear.
Forth rec. 28.02.2010 40 minutes	Child1: female, 5;00 Child2: female, 6;00 Child3: male, at school-age	In a special Kurdish school which is held for three-hours a week for teaching Kurdish as mother tongue. The recording takes place during a 40-mints break. In the school there are about 20 pupils with different

		ages from 7 to 10. Child 1, who has an audio-receiver fixed on his jacket, is with child 2. They talk to each other and to other pupils outside the classroom.
Fifth rec. 12- 05- 2009 75 minutes	Parents: workers Child1: female, 5;2, attends kindergarten Child2: female, 5, attends kindergarten Child3: female, 2;5 Child 4: male, 7;9, attends school	1st session: In the house of the family. 2nd session: In a playground. The children interact with their parents and they play with other children from the community.

→ Total number of pre-school child-subjects: 12
→ Total time of recording: 525 minutes

8. Kurdish-German intrasentential CS: Data and analysis

In this section a general description of the collected data is presented. The data is being categorized so as to point out the total amount of intrasentential types of CS. In categorizing intrasentential switches, groups and grammatical categories are also formed within this differentiation. This part of data presentation provides the data that this study is mainly based on. So the following sections will be devoted to discuss and analyse Kurdish-German intrasentential CS; grammatical constraints and the application of the Matrix Language Frame (MLF) Model will be tested on the data.

8.1. What is not accounted as CS

In the transcriptions of the recorded data some other related linguistic phenomena of language contact could be observed that are not regarded as cases of CS. Proper names like names of places such as *Donau*, names of products such as *shampoo*, or expressions of concepts that do not exist in Kurdish such as *Hausmeister* were not regarded as cases of CS.

Some English items, such as *talafun* ('telephone'), occur in the data that usually occur in monolingual Kurdish. These words, too, were excluded from the CS data and are not regarded as switched words, since such items are identified as syntactic and morphological parts of the recipient-language fragments in which they are embedded. Such English items have been assimilated into the grammatical system of Kurdish, as illustrated in (45) from the data of this study.

Ex. 45

| Child (4;6): Bawa *talafun*-akat | '*Daddy telephone*-does' |
| | 'Daddy makes *a call*' |

In (45) the lexical item *talafun* is an English-origin item which has occurred in a Kurdish utterance but it functions morphologically and syntactically as though it was Kurdish. The item, therefore, can be regarded as an inflected borrowed form and not as a code-switched item from English or German into Kurdish.

8.2. The data

Intrasentential CS represents the greatest number of switches in the data. Figure 1 and 2 shall illustrate the total amount of Kurdish-German intrasentential switches found in the collected data. These switches have been classified and further sub-classified according to the grammatical categories of both languages. Taken from the collected data, samples for each switched category will be brought and then a thorough analysis and discussion will be applied. Furthermore, each of the selected examples of Kurdish-German CS utterances from the data will be classified according to their internal linguistic constituency and for each Kurdish-German speech sample its glossing and then its translation into English will be provided.

It should be kept in mind that the data represents only those intrasentential code-switches that have been uttered by children whose age range is from 2 up to 6, as only these represent the target group of observation. When it is needed, the speech samples taken from the parents or adults of the community will be presented, too.

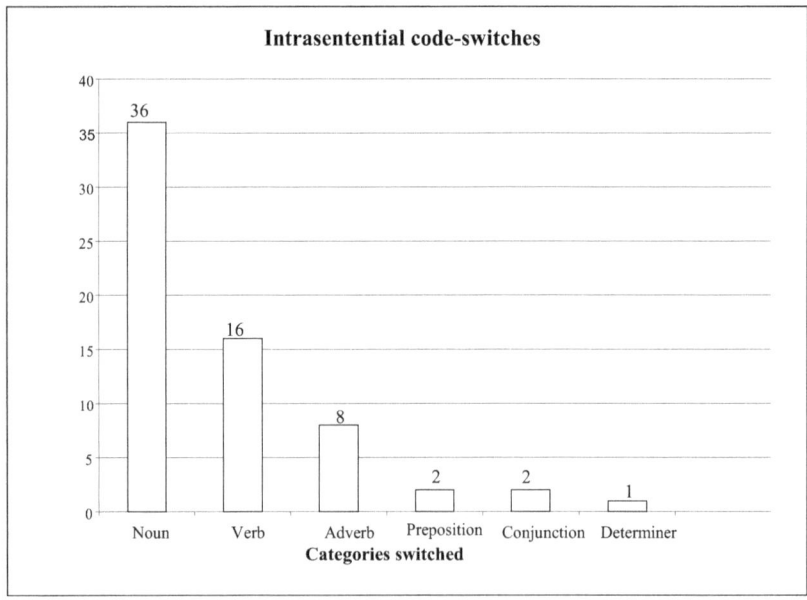

Figure 1: Intrasentential code-switches

Figure 1 shows the total number of intrasentential switches either into German or into Kurdish (65 switches). The figure reveals that nouns, at the first place, and then verbs are the most frequently switched category. Figure 1, includes the number of intra-word switches that occurred within noun and verb phrases, too. The following figure (figure 2), however, shall present the total number of such intra-word switches alone, illustrating their internal linguistic constituency.

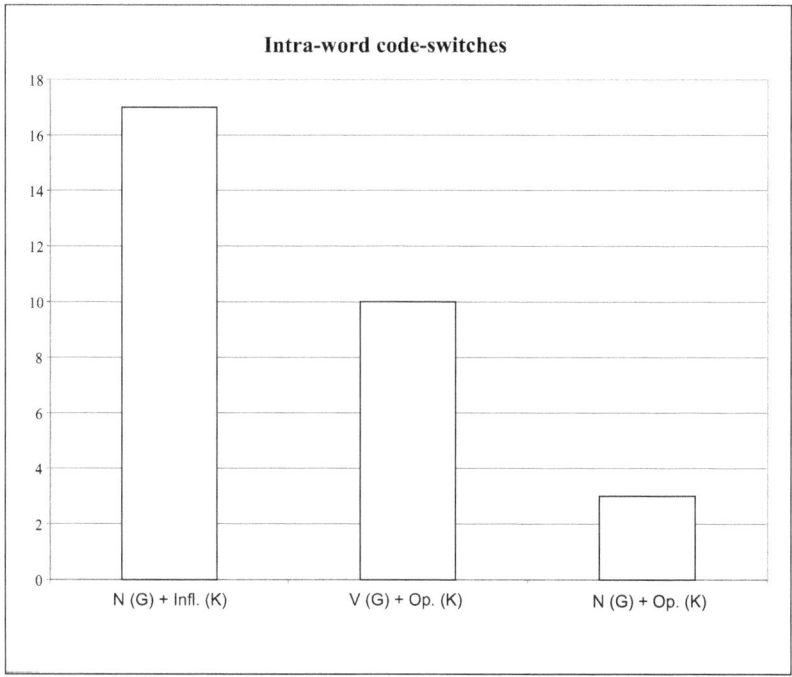

Figure 2: Intra-word code-switches

Figure 2: Distribution of intra-word code-switches {N (G) + Infl. (K): German noun in combination with Kurdish inflectional morpheme, V (G) + Op. (K): German verb in combination with Kurdish operator, N (G) + Op. (K): German noun in combination with Kurdish operator}.

In figure 2, some categories such as *noun* and *verb* have been subcategorised according to the grammatical units of the switched utterances. Generally these subgroups are identical with regard to grammatical categories of both involved languages, Kurdish and German. Hence, grammatical categories have been introduced and in addition to that, each category has been classified according to the language of the given category. In the following sections, these switches will be analysed.

8.3. Data Analysis
8.3.1. Categories switched
8.3.1.1. Noun

As can be seen in figure 1, the highest frequency can be observed in the switching of nouns (36 switches). It accounts for 55% of all the switches. Within the category of *noun*, as can be seen in figure 2, a German noun in combination with (a) Kurdish morpheme(s) is the most popular type of switching (17 switches, 47%), followed by Kurdish proper nouns with 9 switches and German proper nouns with 8 switches which comes on the third position within the category of noun. Three German nouns, however, occurred in combination with the Kurdish operator *krdn* (this will be discussed in 8.3.2.2.). The sentences in (46) are examples from the data of this study.

Ex. 46a

| Awa jiy-a, *glass*? | 'That what-is, *glass*?' |
| | 'What is that, *glass*?' |

In (46a) the German noun *glass* was switched into a Kurdish sentence.

Ex. 46b

| Chile (2;8): *Bawe* was ist das? | 'Daddy what is this?' |

In (46b) the Kurdish noun *bawe* was embedded in a German sentence.

Ex. 46c

Kuwa *glass*-aka-m	'Where-is *glass*-def. sg.'
Wh. N (G) + df. sg. + poss. 1st sg. (K)	'Where is my *glass*'

Example (46c) contains a sentence showing not only intrasentential CS but specifically 'intraword' switching in '*glass*-aka-m'. As the internal constituent structure of the switched constituent shows, in this example the Kurdish inflectional morpheme {-aka}, which shows definiteness and number, plus the Kurdish possessive pronominal suffix {-m} have been attached to the German noun *glass*.

As has been shown in figure 2, there are 17 switches within the boundary of a word where one or more Kurdish bound morphemes have been combined to the German free morpheme *noun*. Appendix (1) shall illustrate all these CS samples.

8.3.1.2. Verb

As can be seen in figure 1, the category *verb* occurred in 16 switches, which accounts for 25% of all intrasentential switches in the data. Among these, as can be seen in figure 2, the subcategory of a German lexical item- mostly a verb- in combination with the Kurdish operator *krdn* plus Kurdish morpheme(s) is the most frequent type of switching (13 switches), as the examples in (47) illustrate.

Ex. 47a

Child (4;6): Komar *warte*, awaika sailikai	'Komar *wait*, look at the other one'

In (47a) the German verb *warte* has been switched into a Kurdish sentence.

Ex. 47b

Child (5;2): *Raka* zu meiner Mutter, schnell	'*Run* to my mother, quickly'

In 47b the Kurdish verb *raka* has been inserted into a German sentence.

Ex. 47c

| Child (5;0): Bas *laufen*-na-be-ka-in | 'But *running*-not-should-do-1st pl.' |
| V *(G)* + neg. + op. + 1st pl. (K) | 'But (we) should not *run*' |

In 47c the German verb *laufen* has been inserted into a Kurdish sentence but the German verb has not occurred alone as a single unit; three Kurdish bound morphemes; the negation inflectional morpheme {-na} 'No', the operator {-ka} 'to do', and the first person pronominal suffix {-in} have been affixed to the German noun *laufen*. Moreover the subject pronoun "we" has been omitted, as mentioned in (6.2.5.1.), the omission of the subject pronoun is a norm in Kurdish.

8.3.1.3. Adverb

As far as the category adverb is concerned the construction of a Kurdish verb in combination with a German adverb occurred in 5 switches and one German adverb has been switched which modifies a Kurdish adjective. But the construction of a German verb in combination with a Kurdish adverb has occurred in only 2 switches. The examples in (48) illustrate this for each switched category.

Ex. 48a

| Child (5;2): Natwane *alleine* brwa | 'Not-can-(s/he) *alone* go' |
| _____ Adj. *(G)* + V (K) | '(S/he) cannot go *alone*' |

In this example the German adverb *alleine* has been switched into a Kurdish sentence.

Ex. 48b

| Child (4;6): Du, dass *yak yak* machen | 'You, this *one one* to do' |
| _____ Adv. (K) + V. *(G)* | 'You, do this *one by one*' |

In (48b) the Kurdish adverb *yak yak* has been switched into a German sentence.

Ex. 48c

| Child (5;2): Xz-a *ein bisschen* | 'Slippy-(it)-is *a little bit*' |
| Adj. (K) + *Adv. (G)* | 'It is *a little bit* slippy' |

In (48c) the German adverb *ein bisschen* has been inserted into a Kurdish sentence that modifies the Kurdish adjective "xz" 'slippy'. Here again the subject has been omitted but the Kurdish inflectional morpheme {-a} indicates the subject 'it'.

8.3.1.4. Preposition

The category *preposition* occurred in 2 switches. Two switched prepositional phrases have been found in the dada, one Kurdish and one German as in the following examples.

Ex. 49a

| Child (4;6): Awa Bawa *mit uns* | 'That is Daddy *with us*' |

In (49a) the German prepositional phrase *mit uns* has been inserted into a Kurdish utterance. Whereas, in (49b) the Kurdish prepositional phrase *legal Ronida u Retub* has been switched into a German utterance.

Ex. 49b

| Child (5;2): Ich muss Kurdish reden, Mama, *legal* Ronida *u* Retub. |
| 'I should speak Kurdish, Mamma, *with* Ronida *and* Retub' |

The remaining intrasententially switched categories include the category of German conjunction in 2 switches and the category of Kurdish determiner with only one case, as the examples in (50) illustrate.

Ex. 50a

| Child (5;2): Nazanim, joni *oder* bashi | 'Not-know-1st sg., how-are-2nd sg. *or* fine-are-2nd sg.' |
| | 'I don't know, how are you *or* you are fine' |

In (50a) the German conjunction *oder* hs been inserted into a Kurdish untterance.

Ex. 50b

| Child (2;8): Willst du *awa* musik? | 'Want you *this* music?' |
| | 'Do you want *this* music?' |

In (50b) the Kurdish determiner *awa* has been inserted into a German sentence.

8.3.2. Affixation of Kurdish morphemes to German lexemes

As it has already been mentioned the category *noun* was switched most often and this phenomenon confirms to other studies on CS in different language pairs. For instance, Poplack (1980), Romanie (1989), Myers-Scotton (1993) found that *noun* is the most frequent switched category in their CS data.

But what is interesting in the data of this study is the remarkable morphological affixation of L1 to L2: the addition of Kurdish suffixes to German lexemes. The data shows that a common linguistic phenomenon of Kurdish-German CS discourse is morphological affixation. In the data the biggest group of CS items account for affixation of Kurdish bound morphemes to German free morphemes.

This phenomenon, namely Kurdish morphological affixation to German, will be further discussed in the following sections. First the data that shows morphological affixation will be analysed and then Kurdish-German compound verbs will be discussed.

8.3.2.1. German noun plus Kurdish suffixes

In the data a considerable number of word-level switches involve the use of one or more Kurdish suffixes attached to a German noun. In this section it will be shown how this process of suffixation follows the word formation rules of the L1, the Kurdish language.

In Kurdish the *noun* is inflected for definiteness, indefiniteness and number (see 6.2.1.1.1.). In the code-switched utterances in the data German nouns have been inflected for definition and number by the affixation of Kurdish suffixes to the German noun, as the samples in (51) illustrate:

Ex. 51

Samples	Internal structure	Glossing & translation
Kakauwa	N (G) + *indf. sg. (K)*	'Kakau-*is*' '*(It) is* kakau'
Rundeyak	N (G) + *sg. (K)*	'Walk-*a*' '*A* walk'
Musikakaye	N (G) + *df. sg. (K)*	'Music- *the-is*' '*(It) is the* music'

In (51) the German nouns have been inflected for number and definiteness and this process of morphological inflection follows the rules of Kurdish (this will be further discussed in 9.3.3.).

Other instances of German noun affixation involve the inflection of Kurdish possessive pronoun suffixes affixed to the German noun as in (52).

Ex. 52a

Tante-*ka-t*	'Aunt-*df. sg.*-2nd sg.'
N (G) + *df. sg.* + *poss.* 2nd *sg. (K)*	'(*Your*) aunt'

The example in (52a) has a complex structure where a German noun has occurred with two Kurdish suffixes; {-*ka*} a definite singular suffix, and {-*t*}, a possessive suffix that shows both person and number. This sample has occurred in the following sentence.

Ex 52b

Child (5;2): Nale aubam bolai *tante*-ka-t?	'Not-say-(she) take-(you) to *aunt*-a-(yours)?'
	'(She) doesn't say (I) take (you) to your *aunt*'

As has been mentioned, Kurdish is a pro-drop language. In (52b) the subject pronoun has been omitted and the pronominal suffix {-*t*}, which has been affixed to the German noun indicates the possessive pronoun *yours*.

In addition to the affixation of Kurdish suffixes to the German noun for definiteness, indefiniteness, number and person another type of affixation can be observed that involves the use of a German noun with the Kurdish *izafe* particle (possessive morpheme) as illustrated in (53).

Ex. 53

Handi-yaka-i daya	'*Mobile*-the-of mother'
N (G) + df. sg. + *izafa* N (K)	'The mother's *mobile*'

In (53) the German noun *Handy* has occurred with the Kurdish suffixes {-ya-ka} that indicate definiteness and number, and the Kurdish possessive morpheme {-i} that links the head *Handy* ('mobile') of the nominal phrase to its possessive modifier "daya" _ 'mother' to make the construct.

This process of Kurdish morphological affixation to German, namely Kurdish morpheme affixation to German words can be traced back to the grammatical systems of both languages. As has been discussed in (6.2.) both Kurdish and German have a rich inflectional morphology. In both languages the category of noun can be inflected for further grammatical categories. Hence it can be argued that this common linguistic feature between the two languages facilitates the affixation of Kurdish suffixes to the German noun in intrasentential switches.

In Muyskens' (2000: 184) terms, these cases of CS can be analysed as cases of insertion where inflections are attached to an imported stem. In such intra-word switches there is the process of insertion inside the word, as the German stem is treated as the equivalent of a Kurdish stem. The German noun has been *Kurdishized*. It should be kept in mind that these German nouns cannot be regarded as borrowed words from German into Kurdish, because these words have not been phonologically assimilated into Kurdish.

8.3.2.2. Kurdish-German compound verbs

In the data a special construction of intra-word CS can be observed that consists of a German lexical item, such as a verb or a noun, in combination with the Kurdish operator *krdn* –'to do' that creates Kurdish-German compound-like verbs as the examples in (54) illustrate.

Ex. 54a

Herz-ek-aka-m	'*Heart*-a-do-1st sg.'
N (G) + sg. Infl. (K) + op. (K) + 1st sg. (K)	'(I) draw a *heart*'

Ex. 54b

| To *gewin*-aka-i | 'You win-do-2nd sg.' |
| S (K) *V (G)* + op. (K) + 2nd sg. (K) | 'You will *win*' |

In (54a) the compound verb *herz*-ek-bka-m consists of the German noun *Herz* in combination with the Kurdish singular suffix {-ek} plus the operator '*krdn*' and Kurdish first person suffix {-m}. However in (54b), the compound verb *gewin*-aka-i consists of the German verb *gewin* in combination with the Kurdish operator *krdn* plus the Kurdish pronominal suffix {-i}.

Such morphological constructions of compound verbs can be found in Kurdish monolingual speech. As it has been pointed out in (6.2.3.2.1.), the Kurdish language has a class of compound verbs that consists of a major category such as noun, adjective or verb plus operator. The operator has a lexical meaning in its own right. The Kurdish operator which has occurred in the data is *krdn* –'to do'. In the new Kurdish-German compound verbs the basic meaning of the compound verb is determined by the German lexical item and modified by the Kurdish operator as it has been shown in the above Kurdish-German examples.

Moreover, more complex constructions of Kurdish-German compound verbs can be observed in the data of this study as illustrated in (55).

Ex. 55

| *Runterfallen*-i-krd-uwe | '*Falling-down*-(it)-done-has' |
| V (G) + Sub. infl. (K) + op. (K) + pp. (K) | '(It) has *fallen down*' |

In (55) the compound verb '*runterfallen*-i-krd-uwe' has indeed a very complex structure. The German phrasal verb *runterfallen* has occurred in combination with the Kurdish pronominal suffix {-i} plus the operator 'krd' and the tense indicative inflection morpheme {-uwe}.

8.3.3. Compound verbs in the CS literature

In CS literature similar bilingual compound verbs have been found. For instance, Appel and Muysken (1987: 126) point out that such a form of compound verb is common in the Indic languages where often a form such as '*do*' affixed to a lexical item from the other involved language, as the example in (56) from Surinam Hindustani-English switching illustrates.

Ex. 56

Train *kare*	'Train *do*'
	'To train'

(Kishna 1979, cited in Appel and Muysken 1987: 126)

The example in (56) consists of the English lexical form 'train' plus the Hindustani helping verb *kare* _ 'to do'. Appel and Muysken argue that the affixation of the helping verb in (56) serves to nativize the English lexical item.

Similarly, Romaine (1989: 131) in her Panjabi-English CS data observes similar compound verbs that consist of an English lexical form and the Panjabi operator '*kerna*' as illustrated in (57).

Ex. 57

Ple *kerna*	'Play *do*'
	'To play'

Panjabi-English, Romaine (1989: 131)

Romaine argues that the construction of such compound verbs has created a number of new compound verbs that has led to a restructuring of the Panjabi verb system. Muysken (2000: 185) emphasizes that the formation of such compound verbs may have the function of vocabulary extension, or may point to lexical loss due to language attrition.

Similar cases of bilingual compound verbs have been found in Turkish-Dutch CS where Dutch lexical items have occurred with the Turkish helping verb '*yapmak*' _'to do'. Backus (2009: 324), for instance, in his Turkish-Dutch CS data found Dutch verbs that occurred in Turkish clauses in combination with the Turkish helping verb *yap*, as illustrated in (58).

Ex. 58

Ali bana *kijik-en* yap-ti	'Ali me *look*-inf. do-3rd sg.'
	'Ali *look*ed at me'

Turkish-Dutch, Backus (2009: 324)

8.3.4. What is special about Kurdish-German compound verbs?

What distinguishes these German-Kurdish compound verbs from those compound verbs that have been found in the CS literature so far is the use of inflections on the Kurdish operator *krdn* affixed to the German lexemes, i.e. the operator behaves like an inflectional morpheme. Moreover, the operator has not been inflected alone as a single morpheme but rather inflectional morphemes have been affixed to the operator and then all together, i.e. *krdn* plus grammatical morpheme(s), have been affixed to the German lexical morpheme.

What all these Kurdish-German CS samples show is that the suffixation of the Kurdish operator *krdn* to the German lexical items has led to reform the Kurdish verb system, which has resulted in creating a number of 'new' verbs which form a considerable part of the Kurdish-German discourse. As has been shown in figure 2, this type of Kurdish-German compound verb is the most frequently switched subcategory relating to the category of verb in the data, where German verbs have been used in their infinitive forms and combined with the Kurdish operator form verbal phrases that function according to the grammatical rules of Kurdish.

Such productive constructions of German verbs plus *krdn* in Kurdish-German discourse are matched by a Kurdish noun, adjective or a verb combination in monolingual Kurdish (see 6.2.3.2.1.). However, in monolingual Kurdish the operator *krdn* does not occur with all verbs, for example *do* constructions are not used with core verbs such as 'go' and 'win', but only with a group of verbs. What is interesting and special in the data of this study is that the *krdn* construction has been used with core verbs such as 'win', which is regarded ungrammatical in monolingual Kurdish. For instance the Kurdish equivalent of (54b) illustrated in (59) below is regarded ungrammatical in monolingual Kurdish.

Ex. (59)

| *To *brdnawa*-aka-i? | 'You win-do-2nd sg.' |
| | 'You win' |

In (59), the Kurdish compound verb '*brdnawa*-akai' consists of the verb stem '*brdnawa*' 'to win' plus the operator {-aka} _ 'to do' and the pronominal suffix {-i}. This construction in monolingual Kurdish is ungrammatical because such a verb stem does not occur with an operator. In (54b) the Kurdish operator '*krdn*' has been used with a German verb in a case where the equivalent Kurdish meaning would not be expressed with a compound but with a simple verb. Thus, while monolingual Kurdish has '*brdnawa*' _ 'to win', the Kurdish-German bilingual discourse has created the new compound *gewin*-aka-i. This compound verb is a new construction which has no equivalent in Kurdish or in German.

What is also interesting in the data is that the operator '*krdn*' has been used with German nouns as well. In other CS data where such compound verbs were found, the operator was only been used with verbs. Romaine (1987: 122), for instance, in her Panjabi-English CS data found no instances of compound verbs where an English noun was combined with the Panjabi operator 'kərna'. As has been illustrated in (57), the Panjabi-English compound verb consists of a verb plus a verb structure, whereas in the Kurdish-German CS data compound verbs can be found that consist of a German noun plus a Kurdish verb structure, as it has been illustrated in (54a) from this study. The compound verb '*her*zek-bkam' in (54a) is a verbal construction built from a noun. Although it is a combination of a noun 'Herz' and an operator '*krdn*', it functions as a verb.

In monolingual Kurdish another very common helping verb is *bu* _ 'to be / become', which allows the same morphological construction as *krdn*. But in the present data only *krdn* was found, not *bu*, unlike in monolingual Kurdish where both forms occur. It is unclear why only one helping verb *krdn* has been used and not the other.

8.3.5. Summary

This chapter has presented and analysed the Kurdish-German intrasentential CS that can be observed in the collected data of the study. First a quantitative analysis of these switches was illustrated. Then, some patterns were analysed from both the syntactic and the morphological perspectives of both involved languages. It has been shown that a considerable number of switches include intra-word switches where Kurdish morphemes attached to German nouns, or German lexical items occurred in combination with the Kurdish operator *krdn*.

9. Constraints on Kurdish-German CS data

This chapter shall present further analysis on the collected data. The collected data will be discussed with respect to the main linguistic constraints and the hypothesis of the MLF model that have been proposed to account for the occurrence of code-switched utterances.

9.1. Universal constraints

9.1.1. The free morpheme constraint

This constraint is based on the distinction between bound and free morphemes. In addition to what has been discussed in (3.2.2.1), Poplack (2000: 222) stresses that the free morpheme constraint suggests that "switches should not occur across a morpheme boundary where a morpheme appears at the end of a multiword fragment in the other language".

However, in the data of this study a lot of number of switches can be observed that clearly violate *the free morpheme constraint*. Quite on the opposite to Poplack's case study where she found no examples of switches occurred between bound morphemes and free morphemes, mentioned in (3.2.2.1), in the data of this study the majority of switches consist of German bound morphemes in combination with Kurdish free morphemes.

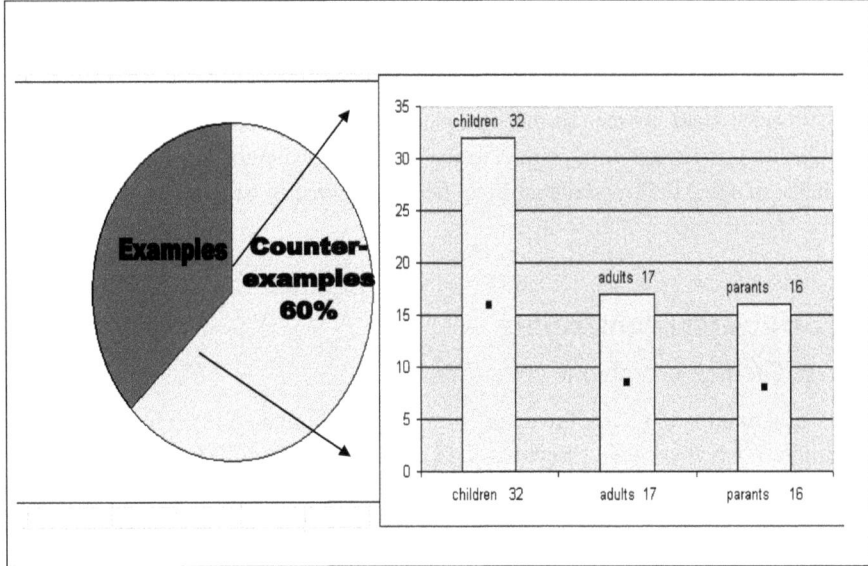

Figure 3: The Free Morpheme Constrain

Figure 3 shows the number of counterexamples to *the free morpheme constraint* in the data. This number also includes the data which have been produced by the non-target subjects of the observation, namely parents and adults whose interactions with the children were also tape-recorded.

As can be seen in figure 3, more than half of the total number of switches that occurred in the data violates *the free morpheme constraint*. From a total of 109 switches, 65 switches, which accounts for 60% of all intra-sentential switches violate the constraint as switches occurred between a free German morpheme and one or more Kurdish bound morphemes. In the total amount of the counterexamples to *the free morpheme constraint,* 32 switches were produced by young children, who are the target-subjects of the observation, 17 switches were uttered by adults, and 16 switches were uttered by parents. The samples in (60) shall illustrate some counterexamples to *the free morpheme constraint* produced by the child-subjects of the observation.

Ex. 60a

Saat duwe, *kind*-aka daxawet	'O'clock 2 it's, *child*-the sleeps'
_____, N (G) + df. sg. (K)___	'It's 2 o'clock, the *child* sleeps'

In (60a) the switched constituent is '*kind*-aka' where switching has occurred between the German noun '*kind*' and the Kurdish bound morpheme {-aka}. Obviously this process of suffixation follows the rule of Kurdish morphology (see 6.2.1.1.1.1.). The Kurdish suffix {-aka} is affixed directly to the German noun stem '*kind*'.

What is interesting in the data is that in most of these switches a German free morpheme occurs in combination with more than a Kurdish bound morpheme. For instance in some cases switching occurs between a German lexical item and more than one Kurdish bound morpheme as illustrated in (60b).

Ex. 60b

Awa *glass*-aka-i mna	'That is *glass*-the-of mine'
___ N (G) + df. sg. (K) + 3rd sg.___	'That is my *glass*'

In 60b, two Kurdish bound morphemes, the definite suffix {-aka} and the *izafa* or possessive morpheme {-i}, are attached to the German free morpheme *glass*. The Kurdish bound morphemes that occur with German free morphemes are very often Kurdish suffixes, especially definite, singular and pronominal suffixes.

Another group of counterexamples to *the free morpheme constraint* consists of switches between a German free morpheme and the Kurdish operator 'krdn' which accounts for 18 switches of this type in the total amount of the counterexamples as the example in (60c) shows.

Ex. 60c

Lachen-na-k-a	'*Laugh*-not-do-3rd sg.'
V (G) + neg. (K) + op. (K) + 3rd sg. (K)	'(S/he) doesn't *laugh*'

According to *the free morpheme constraint* the switched constituent *lachen-naka* would be ungrammatical because the verbal root '*lachen*' is from German, and the affix attached to it is from Kurdish. The Kurdish operator '*krdn*' is not a free morpheme, and hence there is a violation of *the free morpheme constraint*.

Summing up, in all the switches that violate *the free morpheme constraint* 118 Kurdish single bound morphemes including the Kurdish operator '*krdn*' occur in combination with German free morphemes. So the data provides strong evidence that disconfirms *the free morpheme constraint*. Backus (1992:17) claims that evidence against the universal validity of *the free morpheme constraint* usually comes from language pairs where agglutinative languages are involved as in his Turkish-Dutch CS data. The data of this study also shows that counterexamples of the free morpheme constraint rather come from language pairs where languages with rich inflectional morphology are involved.

9.1.2. The equivalence constraint

In the data of this study a great number of switches violate *the equivalence constraint*, where switches occur at points where the relative word order is not shared by the two languages, i.e. at boundaries not common in the grammars of any of the two languages as illustrated in (61).

Ex. 61

Kind-aka daxawet	'*Child*-the sleeps'
N (G) + df. sg. (K) V (K)	'The *child* sleeps'

In (61), the switched constituent is the nominal head *kind*aka where a switch has occurred between the German noun *Kind* and the Kurdish definite suffix {-aka}. In Kurdish, definite articles (in the form of inflectional morphemes) occur after the noun and the article is affixed directly to the noun stem, whereas in German definite articles precede the noun and cannot be attached to the noun stem. But as can be seen in (61), although the order of constituents is different from each language, switching has occurred. *The equivalence constraint* wrongly predicts no switches in such cases.

As has been shown in figure 2, in the data of this study 17 switches have been found between a German noun and Kurdish inflectional morphemes, and all these examples disconfirm the validity of *the equivalence constraint*, because in German nouns do not take inflectional morphemes that show definition.

In the following sections many more examples will be shown from the data that violate both *the free morpheme constraint* and *the equivalence constraint*. Thus these two suggested constraints cannot account for the majority of instances of CS in the data on which this study is based.

9.2. The closed class constraint

In the previous sections efforts were made to point out specific points where switches occurred. However, in this section the data will be analysed to explain and find out which constituents can be switched and why.

As has been discussed in (3.3.1.1.1.2.), Joshi (1989), among other linguists, suggested the relevance of word class in investigating linguistic constraints on CS. In this section, the following hypothesis will be tested on the data of this study.

- Closed class items cannot be switched (Joshi 1989).

All switched items from the data of this study are words from open classes. Only one item was switched that comes from the closed class. As the examples in (62) illustrate, the switched item in each sample is an open class item and there is no switching of a closed class item.

Ex. 62

a) Awe hini *Muzik*-aka-ye	'That from *music*-df. sg.-is'
N (G) + df. sg. (K)	'That is from the *music*'
b) La *glass*-a sharbat axoit	'In *glass*-a juice drink-2nd sg.'
Prep. (K) *N (G)* + postpositional infl. (K)	'(You) drink juice in *glass*'
c) La *park*-in	'In *park*-1st pl'
Prep. (K) *N (G)* + 1st pl. (K)	'(We) are in *park*'
d) To *gewinn*-aka-i	'You *win*-do-2nd sg.'
S (K) V (G) + operator (K) + 2nd sg. (K)	'You *win*'

In (62a), the switched item *Muzik* is a noun stem that is an open class item, but the definite article suffix {-akaye} that is affixed directly to the noun stem is a closed class item and stays in Kurdish. Similarly, in (62b) the open class item *glass* is switched into Kurdish, but the postpositional inflectional morpheme {-a} that is a part of the Kurdish proposition {-la} is not switched and occurs in Kurdish. In (62c), again the switched constituent is the German open class item *park*, but the pronominal suffix {-in}, which is a closed class item, is not switched along with the German noun and stays in Kurdish. In (62d), the switched item is the German verb *gewinn* which is an open class item, but the German inflectional morpheme {*st*} which refers to second person singular and is a closed class item, is not switched along with the German verb and occurs in Kurdish.

In the Kurdish language, the pronominal suffixes express both person and number (6.2.1.1.3.). All the examples in Appendix (1) show more similar cases of Kurdish-German CS where the switched items belong to open classes, but not to closed class. The linguistic constituency of this group of CS samples consists of a German noun which is switched into Kurdish and Kurdish inflectional morphemes are attached to the German noun stem.

However, another group of examples can also be observed in the data that support *the closed class constraint*, which are the German-Kurdish compound verbs consisting of a German lexical morpheme in combination with the Kurdish operator '*krdn*'. As has already been hinted at in (8.3.2.2.) where Kurdish-German compound verbs have been discussed, all of these compound verbs confirm the following constraint:

- "Certain closed class items such as tense, auxiliaries, and helping verb cannot be switched when they appear in the main verbal phrase" (Joshi 1989)

This is illustrated in the following examples in (63):

Ex. 63

a) *To spiel*-aka-i?	'You *play*-do?
S (K) *V (G)* + op. (K) + 2nd sg. (K)	'Do you *play?*'
b) Hi mn *löschen*-na-k-a.	'Mine *delete*-not-does'
S (K) *V (G)* + neg. (K) + op. (K) + 3rd sg. (K)	'Mine doesn't *delete*'

In (63a), the switched item *spiel* is an open class item, but the closed class items {-aka} and {-i} are not switched. These examples are quite similar to the example that has been taken from Joshi's Marathi-English CS data presented in (3.3.1.1.1.2.). Appendix (2) shall provide all the examples from the data that show similar cases of CS where open class items are switched into Kurdish but the closed class items are not.

Summing up, the above examples and all the examples in the two appendixes mentioned above strongly support the validity of the constraint that;

- Open class items participate in CS, but closed class items do not.

However, in the collected data one case of CS can be observed that contradicts *the closed class constraint* as illustrated in (64).

Ex. 64

Child (5;2): Nzanim, joni *oder* bashi	'Not-know-1st sg., how-2nd sg. *or* fine-2nd sg. '(I) don't know, how are (you), *or* (you) are fine'

In (64), the switched item *oder* is a conjunction, which is a closed class item, while is inserted into a Kurdish utterance. This is the only counter-example to *the closed class constraint* that can be observed in the data.

9.3. Applying Myers-Scotton's MLF model to the data

As has been discussed in (3.3.3.), two theoretical constructs underline the Matrix Language Frame (MLF) model of intrasentential CS:

1) The distinction between the Matrix Language and the Embedded Language
2) The distinction between content morphemes vs. system morphemes.

In the following sections these two theoretical constructs and related hypotheses will be applied to the Kurdish-German intrasentential CS data of the present study.

9.3.1. Identifying the Matrix Language (ML) in the data

The MLF model proposes that the participation of the languages involved in intrasentential CS utterances is different. Since the ML plays a major role in CS utterances, it is essential to identify the ML vs. the EL in the data of this study.

In broad terms, as Winford (2003: 141) points out, researchers follow different sets of criteria for identifying the ML in CS utterances. It has been suggested that the speaker's first language is the ML, whereas others suggest that the ML is the language of the main verb stem or inflection in a sentence showing CS. However, from a sociolinguistic perspective the MLF model suggests that a frequency metric will identify the ML. Furthermore the psycholinguistic criterion to be considered in identifying the ML is relative language proficiency. However, as will be shown in the following sections, none of these criteria alone can make a clear-cut distinction between the ML and the EL of the CS utterances of the data.

9.3.1.1. The frequency counting criterion

Regarding frequency counting for identifying the ML, the MLF model further suggests that frequency counts must be based on a discourse sample rather than simple sentences; a discourse sample means more than a sentence (Myers-Scotton 1993: 68). In the following two examples taken from the data, the ML and the EL will be identified on the basis of frequency counts.

Speech situation is given: The conversation takes place at home between a child (2;8) and his father. In (65a), the child starts his linguistic interaction with his father and after a while the child utters (65b).

Ex. 65a

Child: Ich will nur *bawe*	'I just want *Daddy*'
Child: Nur *bawe* will	'Just want *Daddy*?'
Father: Nur *bawe* will?	'Just want *Daddy*'

Ex. 65b

| Child: Schene arwat bo *Kindergarten* | 'Schene goes to *kindergarten*' |

As can be seen, each utterance in (65a) consists of several German morphemes and only one Kurdish switched morpheme *bawe* '*Daddy*'. Hence the ML of this conversation is German because obviously here are more German morphemes in this interaction. Similarly in (65b), which is a single declarative sentence that involves the code-switched constituent *Kindergarten*, the ML is Kurdish because it contributes more morphemes than German. In the data there are several individual CS utterances for which the ML is difficult to be identified purely on the basis of a frequency count as the example in (66) illustrates.

Ex (66): Speech situation: a number of children play at a playground. A child talks to another child.

| Child (5;2): Raka zu meiner Mutter schnell | '*Run* to my mother fast' |
| Child (5;2): Raka *schnell*. | 'Run *fast*' |

According to the frequency count criterion, German is the ML of the first utterance in (66); the utterance consists of only one Kurdish morpheme "raka" _'run' which is a verb and four German morphemes. The second utterance also consists of one Kurdish morpheme, 'raka', and the German morpheme '*schnell*'. Thus in the case of the second utterance, a frequency metric does not help in identifying the ML. But if we take both utterances as a discourse sample, the ML is German. However, based on the prediction that the language of the main verb stem is the ML, then Kurdish should be the ML in (66). Consider the example in (67).

Ex. 67

| *MP3*-ya *Shatzi*, *MP3*-yaka-ya | '*MP3*-is *darling*, *MP3*-the-is' |
| *N (G)* + indf. sg. (K) *N (G)*, *N (G)* + df. sg. (K) | '(It) is *MP3*, *darling* (it) is the *MP3*' |

As can be noted, the utterance in (67) consists of the three German morphemes '*MP3, Shatzi, MP3* and the Kurdish inflectional morphemes {-ya, -yaka, -ya} affixed to the German noun '*MP3*'. So according to frequency counting the ML of this utterance is German, since German contributes more morphemes than Kurdish. However according to the suggestion that the ML is the language that contributes inflectional morphemes in a sentence showing CS, Kurdish should be the ML.

Examples in (65a) and (66) indicate that the speaker's first language will not necessarily be the ML in the speaker's CS patterns; consider the fact that all the subjects of the observation have Kurdish as their mother tongue. Furthermore, (65a) and (65b) show that the ML changes from one discourse sample to another within the same speech situation. In the data many more examples can be observed where parts of a conversation have Kurdish as the ML, while individual sentences in that particular conversation have either Kurdish or German as the ML.

9.3.1.2. Language proficiency

The relative linguistic proficiency for identifying the ML seems to be of limited value. First, measuring proficiency always remains a controversial issue (see 1.3.1.). Second, since the immigrant community under study is not a stable bilingual community, it is especially difficult to identify the speakers' better language. In the data, as has been shown above, the ML can change from turn to turn even for the same speaker. Regarding the young children of the community it is specifically difficult to find out in which language these children are more fluent. Moreover within the community the dominant language of the children is changing from one family to another. This will be further discussed in (10.3.) which is devoted to functional factors on CS.

So as to avoid confusion in identifying the ML, the criterion that is applied to identify the ML of the switched constituents of the data of this study will be further discussed in (9.3.5.).

9.3.2. Separating content and system morphemes

The distinction between content and system morphemes in the data is not problematic. Figure 1 in (8.2.) shows types of categories which have been switched either into German or Kurdish. The content morphemes of the mixed constituents include the categories of noun, verb, adverb and adjective. The system morphemes of the switched constituents include Kurdish inflectional morphemes for the majority of the switched constituents. As has previously been discussed, these inflectional morphemes can be further divided into two groups.

First, affixes which are prototypical system morphemes. Second, the Kurdish operator *krdn* _'to do' which has been suffixed to a German stem. The MLF model (Myers-Scotton 1992: 100) itself distinguishes *do* verbs as system morphemes. And the rest of the system morphemes that have been switched in the data consist of prepositions and articles which are again system morphemes.

9.3.3. The Matrix Language hypothesis

The MLF model formulates a set of interrelated hypotheses so as to predict how the syntactic frames of the switched sentences are set and filled in. In this section, these hypotheses will be reintroduced briefly (for further detail see 3.3.2.), and then they will be tested on the data.

The model makes the following predictions:

- The grammar of the ML sets the morphosyntactic frame for ML + EL constituents. Further from this hypothesis two principles are derived.

1) The morpheme order principle:

- Morpheme order in ML + EL constituents must not violate the morpheme order of the ML.

2) The system morpheme principle:

- All syntactically relevant system morphemes must come from the ML.

The Uniform Structure Principle:

- In bilingual speech, the structures of the ML are always preferred but some embedded structures are allowed if the ML clause structure is observed (Myers-Scotton 2002: 8).

The following examples from the data will be analysed according to the ML hypothesis.

Ex. 68

Child (2;7): Awa *glass*-aka-i mna	'That is *glass*-the-of mine'
____ N (G) + df. (K) + izafa (K)	'That is my *glass*'

In (68), the only item from German is the noun *glass* to which the Kurdish morphemes {-aka} and {-i} have been affixed. This sentence contains morphemes from both the ML and the EL, and CS occurs in "*glass*akai" that consists of ML + EL constituents. It can be noted that the German noun behaves according to grammar rules of Kurdish and not of German. In the Kurdish language, nouns can be inflected for definition and number (see 6.2.1.1.1.). Thus in (68), the German noun behaves as a Kurdish noun that takes suffixes; as can be seen, the Kurdish definite suffix {-aka} and the possessive morpheme {-i} have been affixed directly to the German noun stem *glass*. While in German the definite article cannot be affixed to the noun stem.

Thus the example in (68) obeys the rules of the Morpheme Order Principle because the German noun and everything else in the sentence follows the Kurdish morpheme order, supporting the prediction that only one language supplies the morpheme order. In this utterance, Kurdish is the more dominant language that sets the grammatical frame into which a morpheme from German is embedded. This identifies Kurdish as the ML.

It can also be observed that the definite suffix {-aka} affixed to the German noun *glass* is a system morpheme which comes from Kurdish. This supports the System Morpheme Principle that requires system morphemes to come from only one of the participating languages. Consequently, this identifies Kurdish as the ML in this sentence, too.

The examples in (69) provide more evidence and support for principles of the MLF model.

Ex. 69a

La *schule*-ai ya la *kindergarden*-i? Prep. (K) *N (G)* + 2nd sg. (K) Conj. (K) prep. (K) *N (G)* + 2nd sg.	'In *school*-2^{nd}sg. or in *kindergarden*-2^{nd}sg?'. 'Are (you) in *school* or in *kindergarten*?'

Ex. 69b

MP3-ya, *Shatzi MP3*-yaka-ya *N (G)* + indf. sg. (K), __ N (G) + df. sg. (K)	'*MP3*-is, *darling MP3*-the-is' '(It) is *MP3, darling* it is the *MP3*'

As can be observed in these two examples, all the content morphemes in (69a) "*schule, kindergarten*" and in (69b) "*MP3, Schatzi*" come from German, whereas all the system morphemes in (69a) {la 'in', -ai 'you', ya 'or', la 'in', -i 'you'} and in (69b) {-ya, -ya-kaya 'the'} come from Kurdish. What is interesting with these two examples is that German content morphemes follow the Kurdish word order but not the German word order. In (69a), the Kurdish pronoun subject *you* is omitted and the Kurdish pronominal suffixes {-ai} and {-i} for the second person singular occur with the German nouns *schule* and *kindergarten*.

In Kurdish the pronominal suffixes are affixed directly to the stem to express both person and number. Similarly, in (69b) the German words are controlled by the word order of Kurdish. The Kurdish affixes have been inflected to the German noun *MP3*, and the German article *das* has been omitted. The German glossing of (69b) is as in (69c).

Ex. 69c

| Das ist MP3 Schatzi, das ist der MP3 | 'That is MP3 darling, that is the MP3' |

In the above example, the German language does not allow the pronoun das and the article der to be omitted.

The examples in (68) and (69) provide strong evidence for the Morpheme Order Principle because the word orders in these examples identify only one language, Kurdish, as the source of morpheme order. The examples also support the System Morpheme Principle because all the inflectional morphemes, i.e. system morphemes on the German nouns, and the prepositions which are also system morphemes, come from only one language, Kurdish. Thus, based on both the Morpheme Order Principle and the System Morpheme Principle, Kurdish is identified as the ML and it is clear that only one language, Kurdish, is supplying the morphosyntactic frame in these examples.

The examples in (67) also support Myers-Scotton's recent reformulation of her earlier claim that it is not always the case that the language that is the source of the grammatical frame supplies more morphemes in a mixed constitute (Myers-Scotton 2002: 61). The example in (70) provides strong evidence for that theoretical reformulation.

Ex. 70: Speech situation: The mother shows her child some photos and the child asks her about a person whose name is Zhyan, who appears on a photo.

Child (4;6): *Dass auch* Zhyan-a	'*That also* Zhyan-is'
Pron. (G) Adv. (G) N + *Copule. V (K)*	'*That* is *also* Zhyan'

In (70), two German items, the pronoun *dass* and the adverb *auch* have been inserted into a Kurdish utterance. The lexical item *Zhyan* is a proper noun for a person that cannot be regarded as a switched item. So the Kurdish language contributes only one morpheme, the inflected copula verb {-*a*} affixed to the proper noun *Zhyan*. Yet as can be seen, the grammar of the utterance follows the grammatical rule of the Kurdish language that supplies the inflection morpheme. So in (70) a single item provides the grammatical structure for the whole utterance.

What provides a clear-cut evidence for the System Morpheme Principle is that all system morphemes of code-switched constituents in the data come from only one language, Kurdish. Surprisingly, no single German system morpheme has occurred with Kurdish content morphemes in the mixed constituents, i.e., ML + EL islands. Consider the fact that both German and Kurdish have rich inflectional morphology, and the roles of both languages as ML and EL are not stable. In the data, many bilingual clauses can be observed where the ML is German, as in (71).

Ex. 71: Speech situation: The conversation takes place at home between a child and his father.

Child (2;8): *Bawe* was ist das?	'*Daddy* what is that?'

In (71), the Kurdish noun *bawa* 'Daddy' has been inserted into the grammatical frame of the ML German. Hence, the following result can be outlined from the data

▶ Although the ML changes from one discourse sample to another, the participation of content and system morphemes does *not* change.

In (3.3.1.1.1.1.) and (3.3.3.3.) the distribution of content and system morphemes in the CS data has been exemplified and discussed in terms of closed class and open class items. As has been shown in the previous section, in all code-switched constituents of the data, i.e. ML + EL constituents where both content and system morphemes occur, the system morphemes always stay in Kurdish. This unexpected and at the same time complicated result requires an interpretation which will be provided in the following section.

9.3.4. The dominant-language hypothesis (Petersen 1988)

Petersen (1988, cited in Lanza 1997: 137) claims that the directionality of switching indicates the dominant language. The author, referring to his observation on spontaneous speech from a three-year-old Danish-English bilingual child living in the USA, has proposed the dominant-language hypothesis, which predicts

> "Grammatical morphemes of the dominant language may co-occur with lexical morphemes of either the dominant or the nondominant language. However, grammatical morphemes of the nondominant language may co-occur only with lexical morphemes of the nondominant language" (Petersen 1988, cited in Lanza 1997: 137).

In the data of this study, the directionality of switching between content and system morphemes of the switched constituents has been discussed, and in figure (1) the distribution of code-switched constituents of the data has been shown. However, the following general patterns can be observed in the switched utterances of the data:

1) German content morphemes co-occur with Kurdish system morphemes.
2) Kurdish content morphemes only co-occur with Kurdish grammatical morphemes, i.e. Kurdish content morphemes do not co-occur with German system morphemes.

From these directions of switching, it can be argued that the data confirms the dominant-language hypothesis, which identifies Kurdish as the dominant language in the CS data at word-level or phrasal-level. As has previously been discussed, the data show no cases of switching between Kurdish content morphemes and German system morphemes. Thus the dominant-language hypothesis provides an explanation for why the system morphemes in ML + EL constituents always stay in Kurdish. However, this result does not indicate Kurdish as the dominant language in relation to the CS data of this study as a whole. This will be further discussed in (10.3.).

9.3.5. Criterion for identifying the ML in the data
Consider the example in (72).

Ex. 72: <u>Setting</u>: *The child talks to her father about what her mother is doing at that moment.*

Child (5;2): *Kaffee trink*ak-a	'*Coffee drink*-do-3rd sing'
N (G) V (G) + op. (K) + 3rd sg. (K)	'(She) *drinks coffee*'

The utterance in (72) consists of two German content morphemes "*Kaffee*" and "*trink*" plus two Kurdish system morphemes; operator {*ak*} 'to do' and the verbal inflectional morpheme {*a*}. The example supports the System Morpheme Principle because only Kurdish supplies the system morphemes of the code-switched utterance. However, according to the morpheme frequency criterion, both German and Kurdish can be considered as the ML of the utterance.

What is interesting is that both the German noun "Kaffee" and the German verb "trink" follow the word order of Kurdish, which participates by supplying system morphemes to the sentence that are inflected to the German main verb. According to the Morpheme Order Principle which identifies the ML as the source of morpheme order, the ML in (72) should be Kurdish.

→ This is confusing; how can the ML then be identified?

Such examples as in (72) often occur in the data and the code-switched constituents, e.g. in (69) and (70) provide support for using the following principle of the MLF model as a clear-cut criterion for identifying the ML in the data:

- ML sets the morphosyntactic frame for ML + EL constituents

Thus, in observing the code-switched utterances taken from the data of this study, the language that sets the morphosyntactic frame for ML + EL constituents is considered as the ML.

This principle of the MLF model provides a stronger criterion for identifying the ML than the frequency metric criterion and the other criteria discussed in (9.3.1.). What makes such a criterion more valuable is the Uniform Structure Principle. The example in (72) and all other examples that have been mentioned so far support the Uniform Structure Principle because the grammatical structure of the bilingual clauses in the examples come from only one language, the ML. In the data, no cases of bilingual utterances can be observed that have the grammatical structure of both Kurdish and German. Moreover no cases of ML + EL constituents can be observed that have the grammatical structure of the EL.

9.3.6. Summary of linguistic constraints on Kurdish-German CS

The following linguistic characteristics of CS can be drawn from Kurdish-German CS data:

Morphology:

1) Affixation of the ML inflectional morphemes to the EL lexical morphemes.

2) Word formation of bilingual compound verbs consisting of the EL lexical item in combination with the ML operator, for instance *krdn* _ 'to do' plus the ML inflectional morpheme(s).

Linguistic constraints:

3) CS data involving inflective languages strongly violate both the suggested universal Free Morpheme Constraint and the Equivalence Constraint.

4) CS data involving languages with rich inflectional morphology facilitates affixation of the ML system morphemes to the EL content morphemes.

5) Closed class items / bound morphemes cannot be switched.

6) The ML is the only language that sets the grammatical frame of the switched constituents.

7) The MLF model is universal

10. Functional factors on Kurdish-German CS
10.1. Data classification

In this section the data will be classified according to the interlocutors and their choice of language. This kind of data-classification will help to analyse the functional factors on the CS data of this study.

In table 2, the data is categorised according to language choice by counting the number of turns of each involved codes, namely Kurdish, German and CS that occurred in the data.

The aim is to give an overview of the language choice of members of the community.

Table (2) Frequency of codes of communication

Recordings	Minutes	No. of turns	K	G	CS
1st recording	120	225	89	83	53
2nd recording	180	487	384	17	86
3rd recording	100	178	43	51	84
4th recording	45	181	7	171	3
5th recording	75	217	65	103	4
Totals	520	1288	588	425	230

Table 2 shows the frequencies of turns of all conversations of the recordings. As can be seen in table 2, three different codes of communication, namely Kurdish, German and CS can be distinguished among the members of the community. Figure 3 shows the average number of turns of each of the three codes from the total amount of the turns that occurred in the collected data.

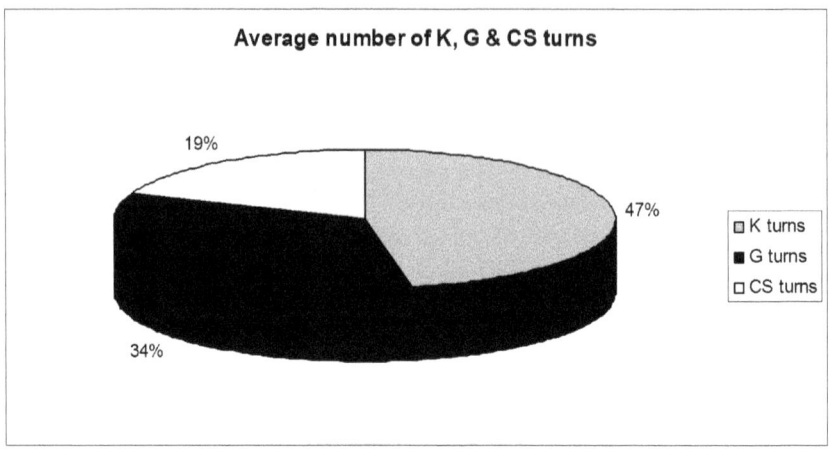

Figure 4: Average number of Kurdish, German and CS turns

As figure 4 shows, the linguistic interaction between the members of the community is either exclusively in Kurdish, which accounts for 47% of the total amount of the turns in the data, or exclusively in German (34%), or in code-switched form (19%).

Table (2) shows that the common codes of communication within the community as a whole are Kurdish and German with a slight dominance of Kurdish. In figure (5) the data of table (2) have been represented and visualised in a diagram.

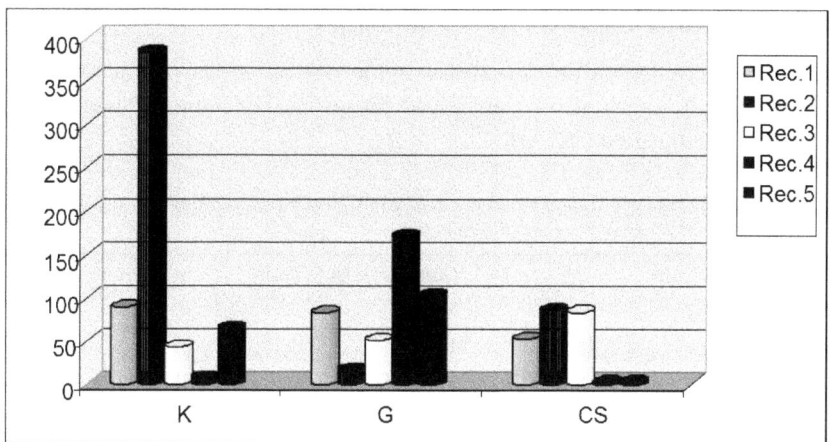

Figure (5) Frequency of the three codes: Kurdish (K), German (G) and CS

As can be seen in figure (5) the frequencies in using the three codes considerably differ from one recording to another. For example regarding the frequency of using the Kurdish code a remarkable difference can be noted between the data from the first and the second recordings that both taken from two families. As can be seen in table 2, in the first recording the frequency of using the Kurdish code accounts for 89 turns, whereas in the second recording the use of Kurdish code accounts for 384 turns. Several factors, however, can be observed that lead to such a striking difference between the data from first and second recordings. First, in the second recording the mother of the children rarely speaks German, and consequently this enforces the children to choose Kurdish as their language of home interaction. Second, the family in the second recording has 5 children and this gives them more opportunity to practice Kurdish as the language of home interaction. Whereas, in the first recording these factors could not be observed; the family has only 2 children and the mother does interact with her children in German, too.

In the following sections the data will be analysed in light of the theoretical discussion on the functional factors on CS presented in chapter 4.

10.2. CS indexing rejection and anger

It can be observed from the data that in home interaction between parents and their children, CS may also be employed for posing rejection or anger by the participants as illustrated in (73).

Ex. (73): Speech situation: At home parents interact with their child, asking him to take the audio-receiver but the child rejects it.

Mother: Ware biyare	'Come, give (it to her)'
Child (2;8): *Nein,*	'*No,*'
Father: Awa abet ba qatdawebet	'This should be fixed on your jacket'
Child: *Nein*	'*No,*'
Father: Ware bashe	'Come, OK'
Child: *Nein, nein,*	'*No, no*'

The example in (73) shows a sample of a parents-children home conversation which is roughly a Kurdish-German interaction. While the parents speak Kurdish, their children keep speaking German to them. The child does not only refuse to accept his parents' request but also rejects to speak with his parents' language by choosing German as his code of interaction. By insisting on saying 'No' in German instead of in Kurdish, the child tries to reinforce his act of rejection.

What is interesting in the data is that in all parents-children home interactions (38 cases) where children utter the word 'No' it has occurred in the form of the German 'Nein' instead of the Kurdish '*Na*'. Even when the rest of the utterance has occurred in Kurdish, the word 'No' always stays in German as in (74).

Ex. 74: Speech situation: A home interaction between the mother and her child.

Mother: Awa Komara	'That is Komar'
Child (4;6): *Nein* awa kosala	'*No,* that is Kosal'
Mother: Na wella awa komara	'No, I swear that is Komar'
Child: *Nein* awa kosala	'*No,* that is Kosal'

10.3. Home language

In figure (6), a further classification of the collected data is presented indicating the interlocutors who are the target subjects of the observation, namely preschool children, and the frequency of each type of code of communication used by them. Furthermore, interlocutors are classified into two age-groups; from age 2 up to 4 and from 4 up to 6. The aim is to show the most common code of interaction used among each of these two age-groups.

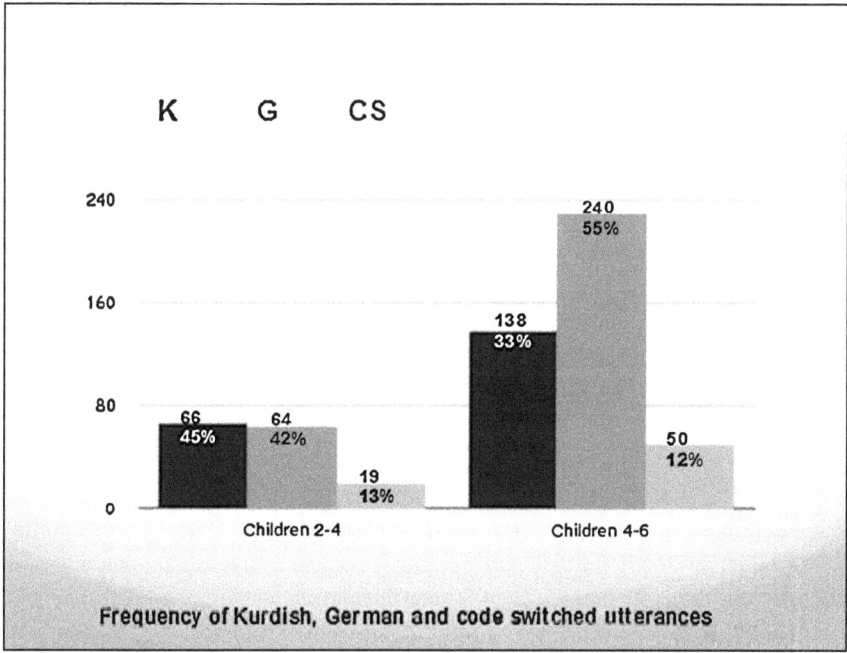

Figure 6: Frequency of codes of interaction according to the age of interlocutors

As figure 5 shows regarding the choice of code of interaction within the community, or even regarding the home language there is not a predominant choice of one code over the other two codes. The data from figure 5 surprisingly shows that the home language of the younger children whose age range is between 2 and 4 is not predominantly Kurdish. As the data shows, the German code which has roughly equal frequency as the Kurdish code also functions as home language for the younger children. However, the choice of language by elder children whose age range is between 4 and 6, figure 5 shows that there is clearly a preference for German rather than for Kurdish or CS.

Hence, it can be argued that this relatively equal balance between the frequency of using Kurdish and German makes CS a necessity. Thus the data supports Merys-Scottons' argument that in situational CS, the change in codes is motivated by the speaker and not driven by the situation. In this case where there is not a dominant code as home language, differences in status between parents- who represent first generation and children who represent second generation of the community- should be the factors that motivate CS. This assumption will be further discussed in the following section.

10.4. 'Children code' versus 'parents code'

As has already been mentioned in (4.2.), a distinction has been made between the concepts of "we-code" and "they-code" to separate and label the languages of a bilingual group of speakers; the former language is referred to as the minority language, the latter as the majority language. However, since the data of this thesis has been taken from interethnic interactions among the members of the community, i.e. no non-Kurdish-German bilingual speakers were present during the recordings, a distinction between the majority language and the minority language as languages of two bilingual communities does not apply to the data.

Moreover, the data from figure 4 shows that there is not a fairly uniform code spoken by all members of the community. More precisely regarding preschool children of the community, figure 5 shows that the languages of interaction for them are both Kurdish and German. It is interesting to note that even for younger children the language of home-interaction is not only Kurdish, but German has also been spoken with roughly the same frequency as Kurdish.

It is also important to note that home interaction between parents and their children, or in other words, between first generation and second generation is very often a Kurdish-German interaction. While the parents speak Kurdish with their children, the children response in German as the conversation in (75) illustrates.

Ex. 75: Speech situation: *Home interaction between mother and her two young children. The mother shows her children a group of family photos and the children ask about the photos.*

Child 1 (4;6): *Was ist das?*	'*What is this?*'
Child 2 (2;8): *Was ist das hier?*	'*What is this here?*'
Mother: Awa Komar-a	'That is Komar'
Child 1: *Und das ist ich?*	'*And this is me*'
Mother: Awa Shene-ya	'That is Shene'
Child 1: *Und wass ist das?*	'*And what is this*'
Mother: Awa mimi Samirau	'That is grandma Samirau'
Child 1: *Das bist du,* daya?	'*That is you,* Mamma?'
Mother: Awa daya-ya	'That is Mamma'
Child 1: *Und da?*	'*And this?*'
Mother: Nabu mimi Samira hat, nanman krd.	'When grandma Samira came, we made food'
Child 1: *Und da?*	'*And this?*'

As can be seen in (75), the home interaction between the mother and her two children is surprisingly, a Kurdish-German interaction; the mother speaks in Kurdish but the children keep asking in German.

Quite interestingly, it can also be observed from the data that the language of interaction among the children themselves is German; in almost all children-children interactions taken from the data the choice of language is exclusively German. CS takes place in rather two situations, first when the children interact with their parents; they switch very often from German into Kurdish, second when the elder children interact with the younger children. It is also clear that the language of interaction among the parents themselves is exclusively Kurdish. That means the first generation speakers of the community are primarily Kurdish speaking, whereas the second generation speakers especially the elder members, as figure 5 shows, are primarily German speakers.

Because the majority of the first generation of Kurdish immigrants arrived in Austria as asylum seekers (see 6.1.1.) they did not come to Austria with the intention to stay permanently, and because the jobs given to them did not require high language proficiency in German, and the majority of the mothers are house wives (see Table 1), first generation of Kurdish immigrants are not enough encouraged to learn German. Unlike the first generation, almost all of the second generation members of the community who were born in Austria, from their early childhood started to integrate themselves into the Austrian society at least through coping themselves with Austrian German kindergarten system. As a result the lack of German knowledge created both psychological and social barriers for the first generation immigrants regarding the German language, culture and society. Consequently this has caused a sort of sociolinguistic gap between the members of first and second generations of the community.

It can also be observed from the data that Kurdish lexical elements occur very rarely in the children's German discourse, whereas German lexical elements in their Kurdish discourse occur more often as the children grow older. It can be claimed that this shows that the bilingual children are adapting to community norms, which disallow the use of Kurdish in German, but do allow the use of German in Kurdish.

Summing up, it can be argued that in the Kurdish immigrant community the three codes in question, namely Kurdish, German, and CS form are kept apart and functionally opposed to each other by the speakers from the two generations of the community. Thus at the level of the community as a whole, in Gumperz's terms, Kurdish which is the minority language, is definitely not the 'we-code' and German which is the majority language, is not the 'they code' as well. Hence it can be argued that Kurdish is the 'we-code' of the first generation speakers, namely parents, and German is the 'we-code' of the second generation, namely children. Hence the 'we code' and the 'they code' concepts differ between first and second generations of the community.

Thus for the members of the second generation, choosing German as the preferred code of in-group interaction indicates their socially inclusive 'we code', while the socially distanced 'they code' is associated with in-group interactions of the first generation. Speakers of the second generation want to differentiate themselves from speakers of the first generation by emphasizing the difference between them through choice of code. The children do not accommodate their parents' choice of language and they distance themselves from it.

The data indicates that there is a sort of generation gap within the community between first and second generations that has been implicitly reflected or even implemented through the choice of language. However, the difficult question which can be addressed is the following:

- How can young children exercise power relations, or negotiate identity with their parents through choice of language?

As this study is not mainly devoted to functional factors on CS, further sociolinguistic research is suggested to be carried out in this area. But in broad terms, what might motivate these children, especially the elder age-group members, to choose German as the 'we code' is the difference in status between Kurdish and German. Kurdish as a minority language has low prestige and speaking it is a sign of belonging to the minority. The children, even in home interactions with their parents, rarely speak exclusively in Kurdish; as has been previously mentioned they either speak exclusively German or a CS form. That means, in a way or another, the children want to associate themselves with a code that has higher prestige than the code used by their parents. This assumption will be further discussed in the following section.

10.5. The unmarked codes of home interaction

As the data in figure 5 shows, both Kurdish and German can be regarded as unmarked choices for the younger age-group, i.e. maintaining two unmarked codes as home languages. According to the markedness model, speakers make code choices to negotiate interpersonal relationships and to signal their intentions towards other participants. Myers-Scotton (1988: 162) assumes that

> "when the speaker wishes more than one social identity to be salient in the current exchange, and each identity is encoded in the particular speech community by a different linguistic variety, then those two or more codes constitute the unmarked choice".

Since each of the two codes of the data, namely Kurdish and German, are indexical of the speaker's positions in the rights and obligations (RO) balance, speakers have two identities and want to make two different rights-and-obligations sets at the same time. Hence, for the younger children both codes are significant and carry equal social meanings and this reflects their willingness for negotiating two different RO sets as simultaneously salient.

The data indicates that although the younger children may systematically differentiate the two codes, it is still not possible for them, or they don't want to make a prior assumption about which code carries the putative 'we' functions and which the putative 'they' functions. So in this case, a possible implicit message indexed by the choice of both Kurdish and German as the unmarked codes, is that these younger children associate themselves with both their ethnic group identity and the mainstream cultural values of the society at large. Although members of this age-group don't have regular direct contact with the majority language, they have daily regular contact with members of the second age-group, for whom the majority language German appears to be their unmarked code and who are closer to the society at large, for example, they regularly go to German kindergartens.

However, the situation of language choice for elder children, i.e., the second age-group is more complex; as figure 5 shows German appears to be the unmarked code for them. The data in figure 5 clearly indicates that the elder children are shifting their language choice from the minority language into the majority language; perhaps this reflects their individual preference for German over Kurdish. In those modes of communication which contain a switch in language, the markedness model explains this as a rejection of the RO set represented by the language choice. The language choice signals that the speaker is trying to negotiate a different rights and obligations balance.

As the code choices are defined as indexical of the rights-and-obligations sets (see 4.3.), the elder children are trying to cope with the RO sets of the German code, and at the same time they are rejecting or opposing the RO sets of Kurdish. In other terms, the speakers of the second age-group are trying to negotiate RO sets which are different from their parents' ones. Through choosing German as the 'we code', they de-identify themselves with the expected RO sets of Kurdish as their minority language. They are trying to negotiate against the RO sets of Kurdish and call for RO sets of German. It can be argued that the possible social message indexed by the choice of German as 'we code' is that the elder children view themselves as disassociated from their ethnic group identity and associated instead with the mainstream culture and its social values.

Again a similar question such as the previous one can be raised:

- How can young children manage language choices and RO balances?

From a psycholinguistic point of view, Myers-Scotton (1993: 88) argues that indexicality is a universal ability and speakers have an innate knowledge of this indexicality or of mental representations of matching between code choices and RO sets. The author further argues that speakers know that a certain linguistic choice will be the normal, unmarked realization of an expected RO set for a particular conventionalised exchange, while other possible choices are more or less marked because they are indexical of another than the expected RO set.

However, from a sociolinguistic point of view it has been argued, for example by Seelye (1992: 15), that there is a considerable relationship between language shift and social change. Seelye further argues that when members of one language community are forced to function either within or alongside another language, both their language and their social life will change.

11. Conclusion

This book has presented a discussion of the linguistic and sociolinguistic research undertaken on investigating linguistic and extra linguistic factors that constrain CS. The study has started out with exploring how perspectives on and attitudes towards bilingualism and CS have changed throughout history.

In chapter 1 it was shown that the focus of studies on language acquisition has shifted from primarily being devoted to the theory of monolingual acquisition to put their equal emphasis on establishing research on bilingual acquisition as well. As has been shown, there are accounts presenting bilingual acquisition as having negative effects on children's intellectual and spiritual growth. In addition to that, arguments were also presented for the claim that bilingualism does not harm the speech development or the general mental development of the bilingual children. A number of studies conducted on the speech of bilingual children have been presented that clearly found advantages for bilingualism and discovered that on various measures of intelligence and achievement the bilingual children perform better than the monolingual children. It was also shown that a widely accepted definition of bilingualism is very controversial and subject to much debate and disagreement. As has been shown, various definitions for bilingualism depending on different approaches have been proposed, which range from native-like competence in two languages to minimal proficiency in a second language. In addition to that, questions about the criteria on measuring the degree of bilinguals were also addressed.

Chapter 2 presented several aspects of CS. In addition to that, the term CS has been compared with and discussed in relation to the concept of code-mixing and some other related phenomena of language contact situations. Sketching some of the pioneer studies on CS literature, frequently used definitions have been presented. Furthermore, the main factors which account for the terminology of CS have been introduced. In the present thesis, however, the term code-switching has been used in order to refer to all cases where lexical items and grammatical features from two languages appear in one sentence.

In chapter 3 a discussion of formal constraints on CS was presented. The chapter started by presenting arguments for the claim that the phenomenon of CS is not arbitrary or random but must follow certain rules. It has been shown that most researchers especially from the 1980s agree that in many aspects CS is rule-governed, and that various syntactic constraints on CS have been suggested to account for the occurrence of CS. It has been shown on the basis of various linguistic corpora that various linguistic constraints have been proposed which describe grammatical possibilities or impossibilities to switch at certain positions in a sentence. However, these linguistic constraints have been found to be controversial and far from being universal; while these constraints are supported in numerous studies, other scholars have identified counter evidence. In addition to that, the Matrix Language Frame Model (MLF), which is designed to account for intra-sentential CS, was introduced, and subsequently its hypothesis and theoretical constructs were presented and discussed in detail in the following sections of the chapter.

Chapter 4 addressed a number of social and psychological factors that involve and influence the occurrence of CS, and presented arguments for the claim that the choice of codes by bilinguals is narrowly constrained by social norms.

Chapter 5 presented a brief discussion of the concept of speech community. It has been shown that early definitions of the concept of speech community tended to take language as central and to focus on the group at the expense of individuals. It has been pointed aout that in some situations such as of an immigrant community in which there is no one dominant language, the relevance of the speech community concept is questionable.

Chapter 6 and the following chapters presented a new study that has been conducted on the linguistic and functional factors that constrain CS by Kurdish-German preschool bilingual children in Austria. The chapters focused on the analysis of CS taken from the collected data of the study. First, a quantitative analysis of the switches has been presented. This analysis shows that children do mix to a great extent during the time span investigated. Several examples of intrasentential code-switches taken from the data have been discussed with respect to the main linguistic constraints and the hypothesis of the MLF model. The results provide evidence that CS occurs at all possible boundaries within an utterance as long as grammatical properties of the two languages are respected. This is in contrast to the predictions put forward by researchers, such as Poplack in the 1980s. As far as the MLF model by Myers-Scotton is concerned, the results show that besides a few cases in which it is not clear what determined the word order, almost all CS instances corroborate the claims and predictions of the MLF model.

The final chapter of the book presented a sociolinguistic analysis of the collected data and discussed those social factors that constrain CS by Kurdish-German bilingual children. The results clearly show that CS can be related to the identity and characteristics of the speakers or to aspects of their social life, and that CS can be subconsciously used to manage conflict when different languages are associated with different roles in a community. The results reveal cases where the *we-code/they-code* distinction, which tends to regard the minority language as the '*we-code*' and the majority language as the '*they-code*', fails to account for the languages that were observed. It has been shown that the speakers of the second generation of the community use the majority language German as their 'we-code', i.e. as their preferred code of in-group interaction, and they regard the minority language Kurdish as the 'they-code' of their parents, i.e. they associate it with their parents in-group interaction. The results support the argument that bilingual children can exercise their choice of the 'we-code' and the 'they-code'. The results also support similar criticism at the markedness model, which also assumes that each language indexes fairly clear values in a given community.

12. Bibliography

Appel, Rene / Muysken, Pieter (1987) *Language Contact and Bilingualism*. Great Briton: Routledge.

Auer, Peter J.C (2000) A Conversational Analytic Approach to Code-switching and Transfer, in: Wei, Li (ed.) *The Bilingualism Reader*. London: Routledge, 165-187.

Backus, Ad (2004) Turkish as an Immigrant Language in Europe, in: Bhatia, Tej K. / Ritchie, William C. (eds.) *The Handbook of Bilingualism*. USA, UK, Australia: Blackwell, 689-724.

Backus, Ad (2009) Codeswitching as one piece of the puzzle of language: The case of Turkish yapmak, in: Isurin, Ludmila / Winford, Donald / De Bot, Kees (eds.) *Multidisciplinary Approaches to Code Switching*. Amsterdam, The Netherlands: John Benjamins B.V., 307-330.

Bhatia, Tej K. / Ritchie, William C. (1988) The Bilingual Child: Some Issues and Perspectives, in: Ritchie, William / Bhatia, Tej K. (eds.) *Handbook of Child Language Acquisition*. UK, Academic Press, 569-643.

Bloomfield, Leonard (1933) *Language*. New York: Henry Holt and Company.

Bloom, J.P. / Gumperz, J.J. (1972) Social meaning in linguistic structures: code-switching in Norway, in: Gumperz, J.J. / Hymes, D. (eds.), *Directions on Sociolinguistic*. New York: Holt, Rinehart and Winston.

Chomsky, Noam (1965) *Aspects of the Theory of Syntax*. Cambridge: MIT Press

Clyne, Michael (2000) Constraints on code-switching: how universal are they?, in: Wei, Li *The Bilingualism Reader*. London: Routledge, 257-280.

Clyne, Michael (2003) *Dynamics of Language Contact English and Immigrant Languages*. United Kingdom: University Press Cambridge.

David, Annabelle / Wei, Li (2004) To what extent is codswitching dependent on a bilingual child's lexical development? In: Ammon, Ulrich / Mattheiee, Klaus J. / Nelde, Petet H.(eds). *Sociolinguistica*, Vol. 18. Max Niemeyer: Verlag Tübingen, 1-12.

De Houwer, Annick (1995) Bilingual Language Acquisition, in: Fletcher, Paul / MacWhinney, Brain (eds.) *The Handbook of Child Language*. UK, Oxford: Blackwell, 219-249.

Edwards, John (1994) *Multilingualism*. USA and Canada: Routledge.

Fishman, Joshua (1972) A Societal Bilingualism: Stable and Transitional, in: Dil, Anwar S. (1972) *Language in Sociocultural Change Essays by Joshua A. Fishman*. California: Stanford University Press, 135-152.

Fox, Anthony (1990) *The structure of German*. Oxford: University Press.

Grosjean, Francois (2004) Studying Bilinguals: Methodological and Conceptual Issues, in: Bhatia, Tej K. / Ritchie, William C. (2004). *The Handbook of Bilingualism*. Oxford: Blackwell, 32-65.

Gumperz, John J. (1968) Types of Linguistic Communities, in: Fishman, Joshua *Readings in the Sociology of Language*. Netherlands: Mouton & Co. Printers, 460-472.

Gumperz, John Joseph (1982) *Discourse Strategies*. United Kingdom: Cambridge University Press.

Gumperz, John J. The Speech Community, in: Duranti, Alessandro (ed.) (2001). *Linguistic Anthropology: A Reader*. USA and UK: Blackwell publishers Ltd., 43-51.

Gumperz, John J. (1986) Introduction, in: Gumperz, john J. / Hymes, Dell *Directions in Sociolinguistics: The Ethnographic of Communication*. Oxford: Basil Blackwell, 1-25.

Haider, Hubert (2010) *The Syntax of German*. New York: Cambridge University Press.

Hamasaeed, Mohammed (1999) *Kurdische Syntax*. Germany: Peter Lang.

Hamers, Josiane F. / Blanc, Michel (1989) *Bilinguality and Bilingualism*. United Kingdom: Press Syndicate of the University of Cambridge.

Haugen, Einar (1978) Bilingualism, Language Contact, and Immigrant Languages in the United States: A research Report (1956), in: Fishman, Joshua A. (ed.) *Advances in the Study of Societal Multilingualism*. Paris, New York: Mouton Publishers, 1-111.

Jake, Janice L. / Myers-Scotton, Carol (2009). Which Language? Participation potentials across lexical categories in codeswitching, in: Isurin, Ludmila / Winford, Donald / Bot, Kees de (eds.) *Multidisciplinary Approaches to Code Switching*. Amsterdam: John Benjamins Company, 207-242.

Jørgensen, J. N. (1998) Children's Acquisition of Code-switching for Power-wielding, in: Auer, Peter *Code-switching in conversation: language, interaction and identity*. London: Routledge, 237-258.

Kaltenbacher, Martin (2001) *Universal Grammar and Parameter resetting in Second Language Acquisition*. Germany: Peter Lang.

Lambert, Wallace E. (1977) The Effects of Bilingualism on the Individual: Cognitive and Sociocultural Consequences, in: Hornby, Peter A. (ed.) *Bilingualism: Psychological, Social and Educational Implications*. New York, San Francisco, London: Academic Press, INC, 15-27.

Lanza, Elizabeth (1997) *Language Mixing in Infant Bilingualism: A Sociolinguistic Perspective*. UK: Oxford University Press.

Leopold, Werner F. (1971) Patterning in Children's Language Learning, in: Bar-Adon, Aaron / Leopold, Werner F. (eds.) *Child Language a Book of read-*

ings. United States of America: Prentich-hall, INC., Englewood Cliffs, New Jersey, 134-141.

Macswan, Jeff (2004) Code Switching and Grammatical Theory, in: Bhatia, Tej K. / Ritchie, William C. (eds.) *The Handbook of Bilingualism.* Oxford: Blackwell, 283-313.

Mahootian, Shahrzad A (1996) Competence Model of Code-switching, in: Arnold, Jennifer / Blake, Renée / Davidson, Brad / Schwenter, Scott / Solomon, Julie (eds.) *Sociolinguistic Variation Data, Theory, and Analysis: selected Papers from NWAV23 at Stanford.* United States: Leland Standford Junior University, 387-399.

Meisel, Jürgen M. (2004) The Bilingual Child, in: Bhatia, Tej K. / Ritchie, William C. (eds.) *The Handbook of Bilingualism.*USA, UK, Australia: Blackwell, 91-113.

Montgomery, Martin (1986) *An Introduction to Language and Society.* USA and Canada: Methuen & Co. Ltd.

Muysken, Pieter (2000) *Bilingual Speech: A typology of Code-mixing.* UK: Cambridge University Press.

Musyken, Pieter (2004) Two Linguistic Systems in Contact: Grammar, Phonology, and Lexicon, in: Bhatia, Tej K. / Ritchie, William C. *The Handbook of Bilingualism.* Oxford: Blackwell, 147-168.

Myers-Scotten, Carol (1988) Code Switching as Indexical of Social Negotiations, in: Heller, Monica / Fishman, Joshua A. (eds.). *Codeswitching Anthropological and Sociolinguistic Perspectives.* Amsterdam: Mouton de Gruyter, 151-186.

Myers-Scotten, Carol (1993) Dulling Languages: Grammatical Structure in Codeswitching. Oxford: Clarendon

Myers-Scotton, Carol (1993) *Social Motivations for Codeswitching: Evidence from Africa*. United States: Oxford University Press.

Myers-Scotton, Carol (2002) Contact Linguistics: Bilingual Encounters and Grammatical Outcomes. UK: Oxford University Press.

Myers-Scotton, Carol (2004) Precision Tuning of the Matrix Language Frame (MLF) Model of Codeswitching, in: Ammon, Ulrich / Mattheiee, Klaus J. / Nelde, Petet H. (eds.) *Sociolinguistica Vol.* 18. Max Niemeyer: Verlag Tübingen, 106-117.

Myers-Scotton, Carol / Jake, Janicel (2000) Matching lemmas in a bilingual language competence and production model: evidence from intrasentential code-switching, in: Wei, Li (2000) *The Bilingualism Reader*. London: Routledge. 281- 320.

Palij, Michael / Homel, Peter (1987) The Relationship of Bilingualism to Cognitive Development: Historical, Methodological and Theoretical Considerations, in: Homel, Peter / Palij, Michael / Aaronson, Doris *Childhood Bilingualism: Aspects of Linguistic, Cognitive, and Social Development*. London: Lawrence Erlbaum Associates, 131-148.

Patrick, Peter L. (2002) The Speech Community, in: Chambers, J. K. / Trudgill, Peter / Schilling-Estes, Natalie (eds.) *The Handbook of Language Variation and Change*. USA, UK, Australia Blackwell, 573-596.

Poplack, S. (1980) Sometimes I'll start a sentence in Spanish y termino en español: Toward a typology of code-switching, *Linguistics*, 18, 581-618.

Poplack, Shana (1988) Contrasting patterns of code-switching in two communities, in: Heller, Monica/ Fishman, Joshua A. (eds.), *Codeswitching: Anthropological and Sociolinguistic Perspectives*. Berlin New York Amsterdam: Mouton de Gruyter, 215-244.

Poplack, Shana (2000) Sometimes I'll start a sentence in Spanish y termino en español: toward typology of code-switching, in: Wei, Li *The Bilingualism Reader*. London: Routledge, 221-256.

Ritchie, William C. / Bhatia, Tej K. (2004) Social and Psychological Factors in Language Mixing. In: Bhatia, Tej K. / Ritchie, William C. (eds.) *The Handbook of Bilingualism*. USA, UK, Australia: Blackwell, 336-352.

Romaine, Suzanne (1989) *Bilingualism*. UK, Oxford: Blackwell.

Romaine, Suzanne (1994) *Language in Society: An Introduction to Sociolinguistics*. United States: Oxford University Press Inc.

Seelye, Ned H. (1992) Teaching Culture: Strategies for Intercultural Communication. U.S.A: National Texbook Company

Wardhaugh, Ronald (1986) *An Introduction to Sociolinguistics*. Oxford: Basil Blackwell.

Wei, Li (2000) *The Bilingualism Reader*. London: Routledge.

Winford, Donald (2003) *An introduction to contact linguistics*. UK: Blackwell Publishing.

Internet Sources

Azuma, Shoji (1997). Meaning and form in code-switching, in: Jacobson Rodolfo (ed.) *Trends in Linguistics Studies and Monographs 106 Codeswitching Worldwide*. Berlin: MOUTON.
[http://books.google.at/books?id=0NxCta42bYC&printsec=frontcover&source=gbs_slider_thumb#v=onepage&q&f=false]. Visited on 13.04.2010 at 01:20am.

Backus, Ad (1992) *Patterns of Language Mixing: a Study in Turkish-Dutch Bilingualism*. Germany: Otto, Harrassowity.

{http://books.google.com/books?id=aHK63_fIIS8C&pg=PA19&dq=usual ly+comes+from+language+pairs+where+agglutinative+languages&hl=d e&ei=lfbWTYPKI8zAswbpwOyXBw&sa=X&oi=book_result&ct=resul t&resnum=1&ved=0CCwQ6AEwAA#v=onepage&q&f=false}.

Haig, Geoffery (2007) Grammatical borrowing in Kurdish (Northern Group), in: Matras, Yaron / Sakel, Jeanette *Grammatical borrowing in cross-linguistic perspective*. Berlin, Germany: Mouton de Gruyter, 165-184 [http://books.google.at/books?id=GzZQGgQOF9cC&pg=PA173&lpg=P A173&dq=verb+suffixation+in+Kurdish+laguage&source=bl&ots=kgrr5 k_S78&sig=buGZ2ySMu7zHvQOVz_OnS4wPis&hl=de&ei=NDwYTsf GMIT4sgbpmqnxDg&sa=X&oi=book_result&ct=result&resnum=2&ved =0CCAQ6AEwAQ#v=onepage&q=verb%20suffixation%20in%20Kurdis h%20language&f=false] Visited on 10.07.2011 at 01:00 am.

Hassanpour, Amir (2000) The Politics of A-political Linguistics: Linguists and Linguicide, in: Phillipson, Robert (ed.) *Rights to Language: Equity, Power, and Education*. United States of America: Lawrence Erlbaum Associations, 33- 40
{http://books.google.com/books?id=NEeotrDahjYC&pg=PA34&dq=Mac Kenz1961,+Kurdish+language&hl=en&ei=JrRBTMa5GIiu4Abo18WRDg &sa=X&oi=book_result&ct=result&resnum=1&ved=0CC8Q6AEwAA#v =onepage&q=MacKenzie%201961%2C%20Kurdish%20language&f=fals e}. Visited on 17.07.2010 at 06:50pm.

Joshi, Aravind K. (1985) Processing of sentences with itrasentential code switching, in: Dowty, David R. / Karttunen, Lauri/ Zwicky, Arnold M. (1985) *Natural Language Parsing: Psychological, Computational, and Theoretical Perspectives*. Cambridge: Cambridge University Press, 190-205
[http://books.google.at/books?id=_QBYTb7z2HwC&printsec=frontcover &source=gbs_slider_thumb#v=onepage&q&f=false].

Kreyenbroek, Philip G. (1992) On Kurdish Language, in: Kreyenbroek, Philip G. / Sperl, Stefan (eds.) *The Kurds: A Contemporary Overview*. USA and Canada: Routledge, 68-83.
{http://books.google.com/books?id=DkI1u4ta5w4C&printsec=frontcover &source=gbs_slider_thumb#v=onepage&q&f=false}.
Visited on 15.07.2010 at 10:15 pm.

McCarus, Ernest N. (1958) *A Kurdish Grammar: Descriptive Analysis of the Kurdish of Sulaimaniya, Iraq*. New York: American Council of Learned Societies.
[http://www.kurdishacademy.org/?q=node/423]. Visited on 22.07.2010 at 08:50pm.

New Iraqi Constitution (2005) Associated Press (Wednesday, October 12, 2005; 3:06 PM) Full Text of Iraqi Constitution,
[http://www.washingtonpost.com/wpdyn/content/article/2005/10/12/AR2 005101201450.html] (05-Mai-2010).

Wikipedia. [http://en.wikipedia.org/wiki/Demographics_of_Austria]. Visited on 25.05.2010, at 12:20 am.

13. Appendix

13.1. Appendix 1

All CS samples from the data that consist of German noun in combination with Kurdish inflectional morpheme(s), uttered by pre-school children subjects of the observation.

Musik-a-kaye *N (G)* + df. sg. (K)	'*Music*-the-is' '(It) is the *music*'
La *glass*-a Prep. (K) *N (G)* + postpositional infl. (K)	'In *glass*-prep.'
La *park*-in Prep. (K) *N (G)* + 1st pl. (K)	'In *park*-1st pl' '(We) are in *park*'
Kind-aka *N (G)* + df. sg. (K)	'*Child*-the' 'The *child*'
La naw *Uban*-aka Prep. (K) N (G) + df. sg.	'In underground-the' 'In the underground'
Handi-yaka-i daya *N (G)* + df. sg. + *izafa*	'*Mobile*-the-of mother' 'The-mother's *mobile*'
Glass-aka-i mna *N (G)* + df. sg. (K) + 3rd sg.	'*Glass*-the-of mine' '(That) is my *glass*'
Glass-eka-m N (G) + df. sg. + poss. 1st sg. (K)	'*Glass*-df. sg. +poss.' 'My *glass*'
Tante-ka-t *N (G)* + df. sg. + poss. 2nd sg. (K)	'*Aunt-a*-2nd sg.' '(*Your*) *aunt*'
*Kakauw*a *N (G)* + indf. sg. *(K)*	'*Kakau-is*' '(It) is *kakau*'
Plet-ana *N (G)* + indf. pl. (K)	'*Plate*-s'
Runde-yak *N (G)* + sg. *(K)*	'*Walk*-a' 'A *walk*'

La schule-ai ya la kindergarden-i?	'In school-2ndsg. or in kindergarden-2ndsg?'.
Prep. (K) N (G) + 2nd sg. (K) Conj. (K) prep. (K) N (G) + 2nd sg.	'Are you in school or in kindergarten?'
La kindergadn-nm	'In kindergarten-1nd sg.'
Prep. (K) N (G) + 1st sg.	'(I) am in kindergarten'
Awa wassa-ya	'That water-is'
Artic. (K) N(G) + Aux. V (K)	'That is water'
awa muzikka	'That music-is'
Artic. (K) N(G) + Aux. V (K)	'That is music'

12.2. Apendix 2

All CS samples from the data that consist of a German lexical item in combination with the Kurdish operator *krdn* plus Kurdish morpheme(s), uttered by preschool children subjects of the observation.

Laufen-na-be-ka-in	'Running-not-should-do-1St pl.'
V (G) + neg. + HV + 1st pl. (K)	'(We) should not run'
Runde-yak-bka-in?	'Walk-a-do-1St pl.?'
N (G) + indf. sg. (K) + HV (K) + 1st pl. (K)	'Should (we) go for a walk?'
Herz-ek-aka-m	'Heart-a-do-1St sg.'
N (G) + indf. sg. (K) + HV (K) + 1st sg. (K)	'(I) draw a heart'
To spiel-aka-i?	'You play-do?'
S (K) V (G) + HP (K) + 2nd sg. (K)	'Do you play'
To gewin-aka-i	'You win-do'
S (K) V (G) + HV (K) + 2nd sg. (K)	'You win'
Runterfallen-i-krd-uwe	'Falling-down-(it)-do-has'
V (G) + Obj. infl. (K) + HV (K) + pp. (K)	'(It) has fallen down'
Problem-bka-in	'Problem-do-1St pl.'
N (G) + HV (K) + 1st pl. (K)	'(We) make problem'
Löschen-na-ka.	'Delete-not-does'
V (G) + neg. (K) + HV (K)	'(It) doesn't delete'

Lachen-na-ka *V (G)* + neg. (K) + HV (K)	'*Laugh*-not-do' '(S/he) doesn't *laugh*'
Schlaf-aka-i *V (G)* + HV (K) + 2nd sg. (K)	'*Sleep*-do-2nd sg.' '(You) *sleep*'
Runterfallen-i-krd-uwe V (G) + Obj. infl. (K) + HV (K) + pp. (K)	'*Falling-down*-(it)-do-has' '(It) has *fallen down*'
Kaffee trink-aka *N (G) V (G)* + HV (K) + 3rd sg. (K)	'*Coffee drink*-do-3rd sg' '(She) drinks coffee'
Au Kurdish *red*naka Art. (K) N (K) V (G) + neg. (K) + HV (K	'S/he Kurdish speak-not-do' 'He doesn't speak Kurdish'
Lagal Pavela *reden*bka Prep. N (K) V (G) + HV (K)	'With Pavel talking-do-2nd sg.' 'Talk to Pavel'

www.ingramcontent.com/pod-product-compliance
Ingram Content Group UK Ltd.
Pitfield, Milton Keynes, MK11 3LW, UK
UKHW021836210426
5322IPUK00021B/320